THE
FIRE
ESCAPE
IS LOCKED
FOR YOUR SAFETY

ON THE ROAD IN THE FORMER SOVIET UNION

MOLLY J. BAIER

ILLUSTRATIONS BY LISA JACYSZYN

LOST
COAST
PRESS
Fort Bragg
California

Murmansk

Rovaniemi Inari

Helsinki

Petrozavodsk

Tallinn

Riga

Moscow Suzdal

Nida

Vladimir

Kazan

Kiev

Saratov

Novosibirsk

Samara

Yekaterinburg

Yalta

Volgograd

Astrakhan

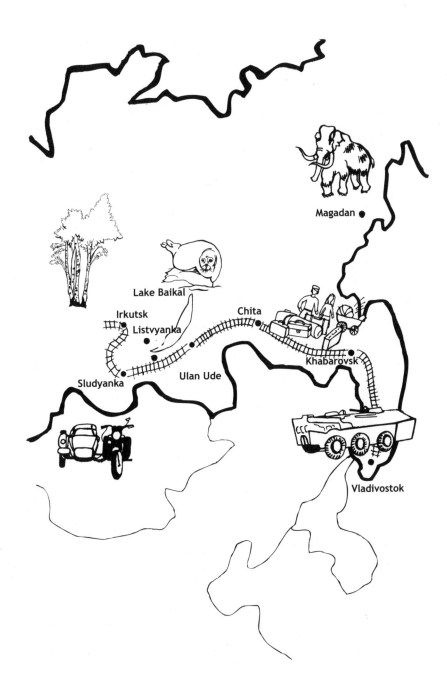

Lost Coast Press
155 Cypress Street
Fort Bragg, CA 95437
(800) 773-7782
www.cypresshouse.com
Cover Design: Chuck Hathaway, Mendocino Graphics
Illustrations: Lisa Jacyszyn

Cover Photos:
Peasant Girl Statue, Western Ukraine: Ann Baier.
Great Patriotic War Veterans on Victory Day, Kiev, Ukraine: Molly Baier.
Peasant Women Selling Produce, Akhtubinsk, Russia: Molly Baier.
Carved Window, Great Rostov, Russia: Molly Baier.
Wooden Church Steeples, Kizhi Island, Lake Onega, Russia: Molly Baier.

Library of Congress Cataloging-in-Publication Data
Baier, Molly J., 1958-
  The fire escape is locked for your safety / Molly J. Baier; illustrations by Lisa Jacyszyn.
    p. cm.
  ISBN 1-882897-65-X
  1. Former Soviet republics--Social life and customs. 2. Baier, Molly J., 1958--Journeys--Former Soviet republics. 1. Title.
  DK293.B35 2001
  914.704'86--dc21   2001038121

Printed on Recycled Paper
Manufactured in the U.S.A.
First edition
2   4   6   8   9   7   5   3   1

CONTENTS

Contents

SIDEBARS

Introduction

From 1997 to 1999, as an American lawyer, I was part of Western efforts to reform the legal system in Ukraine. On long, dark, snowy nights, sitting at the kitchen table of my turn-of-the-century apartment in Kiev while six-legged creatures scurried in the shadows ("like prunes", says Gogol), I pored through many fine technical analyses, by thoughtful scholars, on legal and economic development issues in the region, trying to find the logical threads of a society that Winston Churchill had called, in 1939, "a riddle wrapped in a mystery inside an enigma." By day, on the streets and in the shops, offices, ministries and institutions of Kiev, I interacted with bureaucrats, judges, lawyers, schoolteachers, small business owners, members of Parliament, high government officials, bookkeepers, ticket takers, drivers, cleaning ladies and weather-beaten peasants.

While friends and family back home endured my enthusiasm for the technical issues, they were clearly more interested in hearing about everyday life: the babushkas selling milk fresh from the goat in old plastic soda bottles on the street; the ravenous traffic police; the heavy dark bread sold for a state-subsidized twenty cents a kilo; the swimming pool janitors who jimmied jammed lockers for dripping wet women cowering behind small towels; and the challenges of baking an apple pie in a country where ingredients are measured in metrics and ovens heat to Celsius. All of this became grist for a lively e-mail exchange spanning the ten time zones between Kiev and California.

This book is about everyday life. In the summer and fall of 1999, after completing my duties in Ukraine, I took a three-month solo trip through six countries of the former Soviet Union. I carried a tiny laptop with me. It was my camera, and this is my photo album, filled with snapshots of the lives and views of Russians, Ukrainians, Belarussians, Estonians, Latvians, Lithuanians, Tatars and Buryats I encountered along the way. The Foreword is for those who would like a little background and context before they hit the road with me.

Some of the opinions recounted here are not ones I agree with. But I have recorded them at face value because they no doubt played a role in formulating the speaker's point of view. Because some people shared their thoughts and opened their lives in places where doing so, though Constitutionally protected, can still cause "unpleasantnesses," I have changed some of the names to protect their privacy.

Come along as I traverse six of the fifteen newly independent countries of the former Soviet empire, twelve thousand miles from the Black Sea to the Arctic to the Pacific. Sit at the kitchen tables of ordinary people; follow me into the offices of local bureaucrats; listen in on the conversations. Then draw your own conclusions.

GLOSSARY

Akademgorodok – Science Village, a community in which scientists live and work.

Amerikanka – American woman.

baba or *babushka* – grandmother.

banya – literally 'bath' but generally referring to a sauna, or a sauna, bathing and relaxation complex.

biznes – business.

biznes tsenter – business center. An office in a hotel which provides fax and computer access and similar office services to business travelers.

biznesman – businessman. I am told that the word *biznesuoman* ('businesswoman') exists in the Russian language, but have never once heard it used in conversation.

blini or *blinchiki* – thin, crepe-like pancakes made from flour, eggs, milk, a little sugar and a little salt. A Russian staple, they are often eaten as a snack or as dessert after a main meal, as well as for breakfast.

borscht – beet soup.

bufet (boo-FAY) – a small, dingy café serving tea and snacks. Usually the fare includes hard white rolls with a slice or two of salami and cucumber or a dab of caviar.

cherepakha (cherry-PAH-kha) – turtle.

Commonwealth of Independent States (CIS) – a confederation of twelve of the new countries formed after the breakup of the Soviet

Union. The Baltic states of Estonia, Latvia and Lithuania have not joined the confederation.

Cyrillic – the script in which Russian, Ukrainian and Belarussian are written, and which has been used to some extent for other languages, primarily Bulgarian and Serbian. The Cyrillic alphabet is an expanded and modified version of the Ninth Century A.D. Greek alphabet.

dacha (DA-cha) – cabin or summer home.

dezhurnaya (day-ZHOOR-nai-yuh) – floor duty lady, probably derived from the French *du jour*. The *dezhurnaya* on each floor of the hotel maintains the key desk for the floor, issuing room keys upon the guest's presentation of a registration card. Depending upon the hotel, she will also perform other functions, such as taking telephone messages, collecting money (in cash) for telephone calls made in one's room, providing hot water for tea, storing luggage after check-out time, and receiving a guest's perishable food parcels for storage in the communal floor refrigerator.

Duma (DOO-muh) – the Russian Parliament.

Former Soviet Union – used here to refer collectively to the fifteen independent countries formed on the former territory of the Soviet Union.

Great Patriotic War – the Russian name for World War II.

GULAG (GOO-log) – an acronym for the administrative agency that ran the prison labor camps of the Soviet Union.

Icon – religious painting.

Intourist – the Soviet Union's official state tourism agency, which continues to exist today as a private company. In addition to arranging tours, it "owns" a network of hotels.

Izvestia – literally, 'news', a Russian national newspaper.

kasha (KAH-sha) – boiled whole grains, eaten as a hot breakfast cereal or as a side dish for lunch or dinner. *Kasha* is frequently made from buckwheat and is a staple dish for poor people.

kefir (key-FEAR) – a yogurt-like beverage.

khapach (kha-POTCH) – a Central Asian soup.

kolbasa (call-bah-SAH) – large sausage. Russians tend to prefer sausage with a high ratio of fat to meat.

kolonka (ko-LON-ka) – as used here, hot water heater. The word also means 'geyser' and [gasoline] 'pump'.

kompot (kom-POTE) – a staple throughout the former Soviet Union, *kompot* consists of boiled fruit juice, sugar and water with a few pieces of fruit floating in it. It is sealed in very large glass jars for winter use. It is made with whatever kind of fruit is available, often from berries gathered in the forest.

korpus (KOR-poos) – one building among a group of buildings on a campus or grounds.

kremlin – a walled fort. *Kremlins* were built in many Russian cities during feudal days.

kupé (koo-PAY) – a second-class (four-bed) compartment on a train.

Lada – a popular make of car, best known for a boxy Fiat-like sedan which still appears by the thousands on the streets and highways of the former Soviet Union. See *Zhiguli*.

Lux (LYOOKS) – luxury, i.e. First Class. On a train, *lux* compartments have two lower beds side by side, while *kupé* compartments have two sets of bunks. This means half as many people share the restrooms in the *lux* car. Other fringe benefits of *Lux* include beds that are already made up and, in some cases, plastic flowers and other special decorations throughout the car, according to the taste of the *provodnitsa*.

marshrutnoye (marsh-ROOT-noi-ye) – a minibus that acts as a collective taxi, generally following the bus routes.

matryoshka – literally, 'little mother'. Refers to bowling pin-shaped, brightly painted, nesting wooden dolls which are a popular tourist souvenir and said by some to be a symbol of fertility. (Also available in Soviet and Russian leader version, beginning with a tiny Lenin in the middle.)

New Russians – Russians who have become wealthy since the fall of Communism and are now driving expensive imported cars, building gated homes and, for the most part, not paying taxes. The general population views the wealth of this group as primarily ill-gotten.

nyet – no.

partisani (par-ti-SAHN-ee) – partisans (here, Baltic and Belarussian nationalists) who fought the occupying Germans and the occupying Russians by turns during World War II. Baltic *partisani* were active until 1953, the year Stalin died.

pechenye (pe-CHAIN-ye) – cracker-like cookies (literally, baked goodies.)

pelmeni (pyel-MAIN-ee) – Ground meat stuffed inside pasta, much like ravioli, but served in broth or mayonnaise instead of a tomato-based sauce.

pen-se (pen-SAY) – giant potstickers served as snacks in Asian parts of Russia.

pirog (peer-OG) – baked or fried dough filled with chopped meat or a wiener. The word also translates the American concept of pie.

Platzkarta – Third Class on a train. The word is derived from the German word *platzkarte*, meaning seat reservation card.

protokol – official report.

provodnitsa (female) or *provodnik* (male) (pro-VOD-neat-suh or pro-VOD-nik) – Train car attendant, responsible for checking tickets as passengers board the train, issuing sheets, pillowcases and towels, and bringing tea to the passengers during the journey.

samovar (SAHM-o-var) – a large pot used to boil water for tea (literally, 'self-boiler'). Historically made of brass and fueled with coal, electric versions are now available, and are found in Russian homes in place of coffee makers. The *samovars* on Russian trains are still heated with coal.

shashlik (shash-LICK) – shish kebab, the Russian form of barbecue.

Skoroye Pomoshch (SKOR-o-yuh PO-mush) – literally 'Quick Aid', the Russian state ambulance service. It is staffed by doctors who make house calls.

slyuda (SLYOO-duh) – mica.

Soviet Union – the Union of Soviet Socialist Republics (USSR), which was formed after the Russian Revolution of 1917 and fell apart after a failed coup attempt by hard-liners in August 1991.

Spravochnoye (SPRAH-voch-noi-yuh) – 'Information', a booth at the train station that provides schedule information.

Stakhanovets (sta-KHAN-o-vets) – a worker during Stalinist times who overfilled the socialist plan by a significant amount. Named after Ukrainian coal miner Andrei Stakhanov, who mined over a hundred tons of coal, fourteen times the norm, during a six-hour period.

stolovaya (stuh-LOW-vai-yuh) – dining room.

sutki (SOOT-key) – a 24-hour period. While English speakers might refer to a 24-hour period as a 'day', as in "he was sick for three days", Russian speakers use the concept 'day' to refer only to the daylight hours.

tapochki (TOP-otch-key) – slippers.

tumbochka (TOOM-botch-kah) – night stand.

Turkic – an ethnic group of central Asia which includes Turkish, Tatar (also called Tartar), Azeri, Kazakh, Kyrgyz, Uzbek and other peoples. Turkic peoples are primarily Muslim in religion.

Uzbekistan – one of the former Soviet republics in Central Asia, now an independent country.

Volga – a popular make of car, more elegant than a *Lada*, made by the Gorky Auto Plant.

zayavka (zai-YAHV-kah) – application.

zharkoye (ZHAR-koi-yuh) – stew baked in a clay pot, popular in central Russia.

zheton (zhe-TONE) – a token used in place of a coin to operate a mechanical device such as a pay telephone. The word probably derives from the Italian word *gettone*, which has the same meaning.

Zhiguli (zhi-GOO-lee) – a ubiquitous Fiat-shaped everyman's car, later called a *Lada*.

FOREWORD

"**M**y bag!"

In the late-night twilight of the Arctic summer, the rickety, mud-spattered bus was disappearing among the ugly concrete buildings of Murmansk, Russia with a piece of my luggage still in the overhead rack.

"Oh, I know how to find him," said Tatiana, one of the two passengers who had just ridden 300 kilometers with me over the rugged road from northern Finland to the Russian Arctic seaport. Tatiana worked for a fishing company in Murmansk, and had taken me under her wing to ensure that I found a room for the night in her home town.

We went inside the hotel and Tatiana explained the lost bag to the young woman behind the desk. She picked up the telephone and dialed the bus terminal dispatcher.

"Good evening, this is the administrator of the *Poliarnie Zori* (Polar Dawns) Hotel disturbing you," she began the business call with the customary self-deprecation. "A foreigner, an American, has left her bag on the bus that just arrived from Ivalo...."

Foreigners were still considered VIP's in this backwater military town, and by invoking my nationality she ensured that the dispatcher would give her first class service.

She listened, then hung up the telephone. "I'm sorry, but the driver did not stop at the bus station this evening. You'll have to try tomorrow morning. The same bus leaves the station again at 8:30 a.m., only with a different driver."

I thanked her. Tatiana gave me directions to the bus station. I set my alarm clock, moving it ahead an hour from Finnish to Murmansk time.

Shortly before 8:00 a.m. the next morning, I went back down the stairs (*all* the elevators were simultaneously under repair) and across the lobby. The same front desk clerk was on duty. She cheerfully motioned me over and — surprise! — held up the bag I had left on the bus, its contents intact.

It was a warm welcome to a new town: personal service in a grand old style, just as Churchill had received in Yalta 54 years earlier. (According to local lore, he had commented that his accommodations in Alupka Palace provided him with everything but lemon for his tea, and awoke the following morning to find a new lemon tree standing in the atrium.)

But every stick has two ends, as the old Russian saying goes. When kings and princesses in ancient Russian fairy tales expressed wishes, others worked through the night to fulfill them. The driver brought my bag across town on top of a 15-hour workday. The hotel desk clerk was probably working a 24-hour shift. Perhaps, while I slept, she and the bus station dispatcher had tracked the driver down at home out of eagerness to show their Russian hospitality. Perhaps it was not too far out of the driver's way to return to the hotel, and perhaps he did so out of kindness.

Just as likely, the hotel was in a position to cause ripples with the driver's supervisor, and I, as a foreign guest, was in a position to cause "unpleasantnesses" for the desk clerk, so both went out of their way to help me without being asked. Ordinary Russian workers, grateful to have a job at all in these hard times, do not have the bargaining power to say 'no' to unpaid overtime and other tasks outside their normal duties.

Members of the powerful Russian establishment in the big industrial cities, those who make and enforce the laws, exploit the region's vast natural resources and control most of the capital infrastructure, are also accustomed to the attentive level of service that I received from the desk clerk, the dispatcher and the driver, and tend to drag their feet when there is talk of reform.

The underlings of the elite are foot-draggers too. Comfortably ensconced in the tangled webs they've woven close to the seats of power, a vast army of parasites enjoys the bits and scraps that tumble down to supplement their otherwise meager means. For them, it is a good life, invidiously rooted deeply into the culture, highly resistant to Western prescriptions for reform, and adept at giving the appearance of engaging in one activity while in fact conducting quite another.

Even - perhaps especially - those at the very bottom of the food chain resist change, for the slightest hiccup in their desperate situations could mean starvation. These include workers uprooted from their native villages by the Soviets and now dependent on inefficient, state-run enterprises for their livelihoods.

Westerners in the region are sometimes part of the inertia as well. Though miniscule in number, their impact on the foreign policy of their home countries toward the Newly Independent States can be significant. Short-term visitors, coddled with kindness, bleary-eyed from jet lag and experiencing post-Soviet society through layers of translation and meaning, can easily develop a skewed view of the direction in which money should be thrown, and squander opportunities for progress. Worse, Westerners who spend longer in the region may knowingly surrender their consciences in exchange for creature comforts, privileges and freedoms previously available only to the Soviet elite. As I was stepping off a Ukrainian International Airlines flight in Frankfurt, Germany several years ago, another expatriate turned to me and said: "Darn. Now we have to follow the rules like everyone else." He was only half joking.

No one feels obliged to pay taxes, and much of what is collected is administered without adequate checks and balances, leaving essential services under-funded and leaving under-paid bureaucrats to use their offices for private gain.

Among the Newly Independent States described in this book, only the tiny Baltics, clinging to the northern edge of Europe between Poland and Saint Petersburg, have mustered the critical mix of means and motivation to break free of this "locked circle." Estonia, Latvia and Lithuania, formerly independent countries with long histories of international commerce, were forcibly annexed into the

Soviet Union in World War II. Their deep water ports provide ready access to world markets, and their majority non-Slavic populations, which were robbed, deported to Siberia and partially annihilated by the Communist regime, have no identity crisis over their clean break with the recent past. To most Balts, working toward joining the European Union makes perfect sense.

The newly independent Slavic states, however, are having a much rockier time choosing and implementing a future direction. In addition to the forces described above which are not helping — or are even actively blocking — legal and economic reform, the attitude of the general Slavic population about moving away from the past (and, if so, how fast and toward what) is mixed. For a significant number, particularly the young, well-educated and upwardly mobile, developing business and computer skills and working with Western companies is the road to a prosperous future. Cash and carry trading in food items, clothing and fast-moving consumer goods is a popular new way of making a living. But many of the movers and shakers are emigrating or are too busy making money in the shadow economy to care much about politics. This alleviates pressure for reform. One talented twenty-something told me that less than ten per cent of her school class had remained in Ukraine after graduation.

Others shy away from private enterprise simply because it is unfamiliar to them. For the many who have no parent, grandparent, aunt or uncle who has run or worked in a small business, there is no role model from whom to absorb the skills needed to step confidently into this arena. The same barrier exists with respect to the absorption of democracy-related skills and attitudes, such as informing oneself on political issues and exercising one's voting rights. It will take a long time for these concepts to take root and grow to be second nature.

For others, capitalism is immoral. (Indeed, many in the West would be hard pressed to disagree if their only experience with capitalism were with the post-Soviet brand: an economic free-for-all in which competition is squelched in hideous ways, prices soar, and there is such an excess of labor that some are willing to work for 25 cents a day.) The appearance of Mafia-style business and chaotic economic change in Russia and Ukraine has coincided with the appearance of Westerners preaching democracy and capitalism in the same breath, leaving some newly-impoverished Russians and Ukrainians with the impression of a causal connection between Western influence and current problems. (Belarus has seen far fewer Western advisers and far less change.)

For still others, embracing the prevailing Western way of life means letting go of something elusive, hard to define, yet deep within their Slavic souls — a different-ness which millions felt strongly enough to fight and die for as a great counterweight to the German empire in World War II, which Russians call the Great Patriotic War. One characteristic of this separateness is a sense that things "for the soul" such as friendship, kindness and religion are more valuable than economic wealth.

Finally, a fundamental factor cooling the Slavic embrace of Western-style capitalism and participatory democracy is the semi-self-sufficiency of the people. Since the Industrial Revolution, Russians, Ukrainians, Belarussians and the ethnic minorities living on the same territory have lived closer to the land than their counterparts in Western (and particularly Northern) Europe. (By 1850, half of Britain's population lived in cities; as of 1914, 90% of Russians still lived on the land, and more than a quarter still do.) The strength of these people against corrupt and inefficient government is not their ability to organize against it (whether by lobbying or revolution.) Rather, their strength lies in their ability to ignore their governments by withdrawing into their countries' enormous back yards. They hunt, fish, trap furs, gather mushrooms, pick berries, raise chickens, dig potatoes and grow vegetables, quietly living out their lives largely outside any political system. They trade in small ways for basic necessities, beneath the radar screens of the voracious tax inspectors. They extract whatever value they can from the crippled Soviet-built infrastructure. (Unemployed urban hunters and gatherers scavenge and prey in much less romantic ways than rural ones, walking off with anything that isn't bolted down and even cutting live electric and telephone lines to sell the wire for scrap.) Illness is common, life expectancies are short, and caring for each other during the precious time they have together is a much higher calling than rendering unto Caesar, for Caesar does not reciprocate with essential social services.

Even among city dwellers with regular jobs, survival skills born in the ancient past and cultivated during the days of Communist maldistribution are being further honed as the central systems continue to disintegrate. They tend to live far less capital-intensive lives than their Western counterparts, doing business in person, making meals from scratch, repairing their own broken-down cars, strolling in parks for weekend entertainment or escaping to their country garden plots to dig in the rich black earth and put up winter preserves.

Of course, not everyone is satisfied with a quiet life of inaction, and significant changes have taken place. Individuals throughout the region who have been kicked in the teeth one too many times are chafing (if not seething), investigative journalists are testing their wings (though finding it difficult to make a living at it), and small numbers of dedicated intellectuals are working to modernize the legal system. Western Ukrainians, who were under Polish domination until their annexation into the Soviet Union in World War II, are eager to maintain freedom from the Russian yoke. Crimean Tatars are returning to their homeland from Siberian exile and building new mosques. In major Russian and Ukrainian cities, a Brezhnev-era time traveler would notice immediately that the building-top signs praising the Socialist Revolution have been replaced by billboards advertising imported electronic goods; that Internet service providers have set up shop; that packaged Western foodstuffs and toiletries are available at thousands of open-air stalls; and that once-dusty state storefronts on the main boulevards are now occupied by glitzy Yves Rocher and Benetton boutiques. But the changes recede as one leaves the city centers and major towns, gradually scraping up against ancient forces of inertia and the daily struggle for survival until, in the byways of the countryside, all change comes to a halt and life flows on as it has for centuries, with horse-drawn carts and backbreaking manual labor, and without plumbing or electricity.

For those who fend for themselves much of the time, government is semi-irrelevant and a nuisance. In this regard, many Slavs have much in common with the rugged individuals whose hearts are in rural and frontier America. Indeed, although there were strains due to Western bombing in Yugoslavia, there is generally a broad-based warmth toward Americans that extends far beyond the cosmopolitan young people who are wired into the Information Age.

The semi-self-sufficient life that has given many the luxury of ignoring the activities of their legislators (just as the legislators have ignored the citizens) cannot last. For those still living off the land, environmental damage and depletion of natural resources will gradually create the need for more interdependence. Those who are currently getting by in their Soviet-built apartments will need to assemble capital for new construction as the buildings crumble and collapse. Highways, heating plants, drinking water systems and other physical infrastructure need attention on a scale that individuals and families cannot address for themselves, and which will be difficult even for government to address without better accountability in the use of public funds. Factories will need to attract capital for new assembly lines. The small-time trading which brings Western manufactured products to the sea of tiny kiosks is highly labor-intensive, and will continue to take a toll on health and family life. Invisible hands more powerful than Adam Smith's are also at work in the economy, exacting additional tolls. To become competitive in a world where even basic commodities are produced or extracted with modern technology, manufacturers and entrepreneurs in the former Soviet Union will need to assemble teams of co-workers with specialized skills their family members and close friends do not have. They will need to devise ways of rewarding creative labor, to replace the old, heavy-handed ways of coercing manual labor; and they will need to be able to send their goods to distant strangers with confidence of getting paid.

To address these problems, Russians, Ukrainians and Belarussians will need a stronger *legal system*. (This should not to be confused with a stronger *state*, for strength can be based upon little more than brute force.) The need will become more pressing as time passes.

As I traveled through the former Soviet Union, I paid close attention to the attitudes of the people toward the law and their government. As a Russian-speaking Western lawyer with a briefcase full of local law books, I was also in a position to offer an outsider's perspective to those I met. Frequently, I challenged those I encountered to think about the law in ways they had not before. Sometimes I tested the bounds of the corrupt systems in daring ways, using the 1993 Russian Constitution as an example and myself — a foreigner — as a test case. The gap between current mindsets and those needed to address today's problems is enormous.

Civil rights is a troubled area. Though all people are theoretically equal under the written law, in practice one's rights and obligations depend very much on one's nationality, ethnicity and, within the large ethnic Russian population itself, one's social status. (Half the population was in bonded serfdom until emancipation in 1861.) *Perestroika* — literally "Reconstruction," and its aftermath have much in common with the period in American history after the Civil War and the century that followed: laws written in a capital city hundreds or even thousands of miles away, idealistically proclaiming equal rights for all, are not finding their way to rural areas. Or, if they do, the laws are not leaping off the pages and into the hearts and minds of the local power-brokers. Even the capital cities are falling far short. The social service departments in Moscow intentionally neglect to provide services for those not registered to live in the city. In Kiev, a member of my staff failed to appear for work one day. She had developed an urgent stomach ailment and ridden 15 hours on the train to her home town, where, due to her status as a local resident, she was allowed to see a government doctor for free.

The have-nots on the other side of the often-invisible but very real "color line" likewise do not support the new legal system, either in making tax payments or in respecting the new laws (which are often disjointed and preferential to certain groups.) They were told before that a glorious future — Communism — awaited them if they would only put their shoulder to the wheel. Exhausted by decades of broken promises, most have more important things to focus on, like survival.

In all of this, foreigners are in a particularly strange position. Presumed equal under the Constitution, in practice they are simultaneously treated as super-first class citizens (like the Russian elite) and second-class citizens. They are often provided with the best, but in a holdover from the institutionalized discrimination of Soviet days, they are still sometimes segregated and are frequently charged a higher price for identical accommodations, whether for a hotel room in Irkutsk, a museum tour in Murmansk or an airline seat in Odessa.

Such double standards, which are informally (and illegally) applied to many locals as well, in many contexts, are a problem. Singling someone out for special treatment is as odious as negative discrimination, because better treatment for one person means, in every case, worse treatment for others. It is particularly invidious when it is accorded to those in positions of influence, for it discourages them from supporting reforms. Further, making it more expensive for some (including foreigners) to travel and conduct business inhibits free market competition, raising the price of goods for all (which, the local monopolists might chuckle, is precisely the point.)

While it is disheartening to see that institutionalized discrimination continues to be taken for granted in many parts of the former Soviet Union, we can draw hope from the fact that America, with its own troubled civil rights past, has made progress through sustained effort on this front, along with other aspects of the rule of law. It is possible for the Slavic states to do the same, with respect to both their class-based societies and the many other legal and economic challenges they face.

Whether civil rights or contract rights, the legal infrastructure cannot be strengthened without the support of the citizens, and a high degree of *voluntary* compliance is essential to *democratic* enforcement of laws and *affordable* enforcement of contracts. It will take a long, long time before the government and the people are able to work together constructively, given the chasm of distrust on one side and disregard on the other. The citizens of the region will turn away from their well-worn paths only when the oppressors and the oppressed (who sometimes reverse roles in different contexts) each have more to gain than to lose by cooperating in new ways, and when the barriers to such cooperation are low. Even under the best of circumstances, this will happen only incrementally, and may happen for different regions, cities and individuals at different times. The rugged individuals, for example, may voluntarily comply with laws and contractual obligations when they can no longer support themselves by reciprocating only with close friends and family, and when the government is providing concrete social services proportionate with taxation.

Things won't get better by themselves, and motivation must come primarily from within. The pain will be less if citizens decide to join the system and improve it, and cease exploiting and ignoring it, while they have some increment of extra food and housing and health to participate constructively in the political process and to weather the necessary changes. Outsiders can help through sustained contact and dialog at all levels of society and through many media and person-to-person contacts.

THE
FIRE ESCAPE IS LOCKED
FOR YOUR SAFETY

Part 1

UKRAINE AND
BELARUS

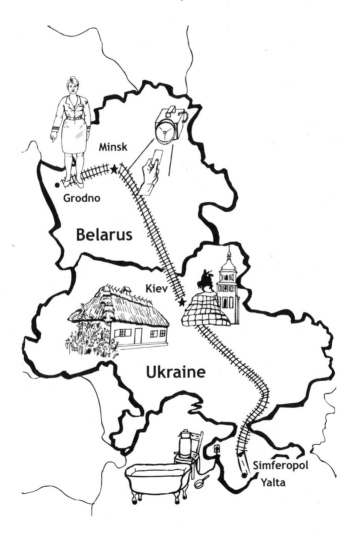

UKRAINE

CHAPTER 1

THE TWELVE THOUSAND MILE JOURNEY BEGINS

Yalta, Ukraine, on the Crimean Peninsula, June 30.

"Let's sit down for the trip," Yuri suggested.

It was an old Russian custom to have a moment of silence before starting off on a journey.

Yuri gave me his fine wooden abacus[1] as a memento, then walked me to the road, flagged down an acquaintance who was driving to the train station in Simferopol, and waved good-bye.

"I'll never forget you," he said. "I'll leave your room exactly as you left it for one day. That's for good luck."

Yuri was nearly seventy and full of stories, homespun wit and wisdom. I had spent three wonderful days between his apartment in a hamlet on the rugged Black Sea coast and the stony beach below, swimming in the gentle waves and looking down at the round purple jellyfish[2] bobbing in the clear water beneath me.

Of course I had had to try everything in his pantry: *ablondzhiri,*

---

1. Hand calculators are appearing in more and more shops, but many state-owned grocery stores in the former Soviet Union still use these ancient counting devices to add up the cost of purchases.

2. The Russian word for jellyfish is *meduza,* after the mythological Greek creature whose hair was of serpents. There was a substantial Greek influence on the southern coast of Ukraine in ancient times.

3

a pepper and eggplant chutney, delicious on dark Ukrainian Bread; this year's pickles, still salting themselves in a huge glass jar on the counter, flavored with cloves of garlic, oak leaves and madrone bark; home-made fruit syrups of various flavors, red and golden, the consistency of honey, some with lemon slices floating in them, others with currants. We drizzled the syrup on top of home-baked sugar cookies and ate them with tea.

"Take a bath tonight," Yuri warned when I arrived. "We have hot water only on weekends and holidays now."[3]

This turned out not to be quite true on two accounts.

First, Yuri, who had been an electrician for one of the many *sanatoria*[4] dotting the coastline before he retired, had made his own hot water heater from an aluminum milk can. It heated about 15 gallons in an hour, through a coil installed in the bottom. It was sitting on an old wooden chair next to the tub. A small saucepan served as a ladle.

Second, Monday arrived and the hot water continued to flow. Monday, it turned out, was a holiday – the third anniversary of the Ukrainian Constitution. Yuri pointed out that there had been a lot of constitutions in the past and he wasn't sure any of them had ever done any good. But he allowed, with a wink, that hot water on Constitution Day was a concrete benefit to the People that the present Constitution had apparently made possible.

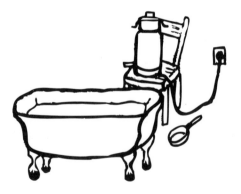

---

3. See sidebar *Water Shortages,* page 5.

4. See sidebar *Sanatoria on the Black Sea,* page 7.

Water Shortages

The Crimean peninsula, which juts southward into the Black Sea at the same latitude as northern Italy, has a hot, dry, Mediterranean climate. Fresh water of any temperature is in short supply and was delivered to Yuri's apartment only intermittently. Yuri kept buckets of water in reserve.

Nearby sanatoria for the well-connected elite, however, had regular water supply. During my stay, the beach showers on the public side of the promenade emitted only a dry sucking noise early in the morning. At the same time of day, water gushed from the showers on the side of the promenade reserved for vacationers from the Ukrainian Ministry of Justice, reachable through a gate guarded by an elderly duty man wearing a red armband, or by a long swim among the jellyfish.

Yuri, an ethnic Russian, had lived in the Crimea for decades. He viewed the Ukrainian people – neighbors and fellow Slavs – as one with the Russians. He shook his head in puzzlement over their desire for independence from the Motherland. But it wasn't an issue he lost sleep over. Daily activity in the sunset of his life centered around eating, sleeping, recounting ancient Russian history and, most of all, playing with the cat that had walked into his life a year earlier through the open first floor window.

"I'm in pain," he explained, stroking the cat's head gently. "I need an operation and cannot afford it. But when I lie down with her on top of me, somehow the pain goes away."

Yuri's neighbor, Ina, dropped in to pay for a long distance call she had made from Yuri's phone. She stayed for tea. A few years earlier, Ina's brother had needed surgery, too. They had scraped together the forty dollars needed for the surgeon's fee, but the operation had not gone well and he was now a vegetable.

When Ukraine became independent in the early '90's, Ina and her husband were excited about the possibility of setting up their own small business. But after finding a suitable storefront and investing a great deal of money to remodel it, they were tricked out of the premises.

"Why not bring a lawsuit?"

"I wish we could," said Ina, "but doing so could cause us difficulties in the community." Her husband had a good position in the civil service. It would be put in jeopardy by filing a suit. "'Just mind your business and don't complain,' they told us."

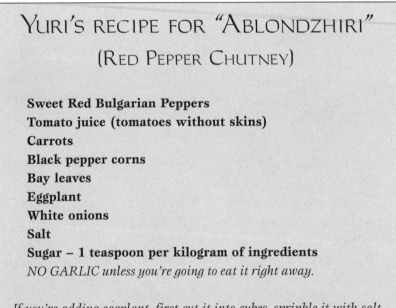

YURI'S RECIPE FOR "ABLONDZHIRI"
(RED PEPPER CHUTNEY)

Sweet Red Bulgarian Peppers
Tomato juice (tomatoes without skins)
Carrots
Black pepper corns
Bay leaves
Eggplant
White onions
Salt
Sugar – 1 teaspoon per kilogram of ingredients
NO GARLIC unless you're going to eat it right away.

If you're adding eggplant, first cut it into cubes, sprinkle it with salt, mix, and lay it in a strainer for two hours. Then cook it a little in the oven until it turns gray. Meanwhile, grate the carrots and chop the onions. Cook the carrots a little. Clean the peppers of seeds and stems, slice them into small pieces and grill them in sunflower oil. Use oil that has been prepared in the traditional peasant manner, i.e. the seeds for which have been roasted a little before pressing, which gives the oil a nutty flavor. Add the remaining ingredients and sauté.

Sanatoria on the Black Sea

Soon after the Russian Revolution of 1917, the Communists gained a public relations coup by sending workers suffering from tuberculosis to stay in the gentry's former vacation palaces on the Black Sea coast, which then came to be known as sanatoria. In subsequent years, as the area became a playground for the Soviet elite, many resorts retained strong medicinal overtones as places for lengthy "rest cures" in the Central European tradition. They are staffed with doctors and nurses, and the more well-to-do resorts have imported American medical equipment. (American and German equipment is locally perceived to be the best.)

A summer sanatorium holiday is a much-needed respite for many burn-the-candle-at-both-ends officials after a year of hard living (including hard drinking and heavy eating) in the frozen northern cities. Younger, healthier vacationers can also find medical justification for a month-long rest. One young government clerk from Kiev, following her arrival screening by the medical staff, was prescribed a "wine cure." She was ordered to drink several glasses of wine a day during her stay. Many other vacationers – with or without prescription – were curing themselves with much stronger drink.

Sanatoria tend to be "owned" and operated by particular government ministries and trade unions for exclusive use by their own workers. Perhaps the most exclusive of all, for high government officials, is at Foros, on the twisted road between Yalta and the military port of Sevastopol. (Soviet Premier Gorbachev was vacationing at Foros during the August 1991 coup.) Privileged children can attend the flagship Young Pioneer camp Artek, on the coast just east of Yalta. Field trips for the campers from Artek include a police escort, complete with lights and sirens.

Since the breakup of the Soviet Union, some sanatoria have fared financially better than others. Those still able to siphon money from the state budget are beautifully kept with well-groomed gardens. The coal miners' sanatorium, which I found up the side of a steep, remote hill with the help of a Ukrainian friend who had vacationed there as a child, was a mess of broken concrete choked in vines.

Kiev, Ukraine, July 1.

It took fifteen hours on the train from Simferopol to reach the capital city of Kiev, Ukraine. As we traveled along the bank of the Dnieper River, my train compartment-mates spread newspaper on the small table by the window and chewed on smoked, salted fish bought from villagers, carefully sorting out the tiny, translucent bones and washing down the fish with bottled beer.

The following day, I sent four big bags of possessions home, the remnants of my two-year stay in Kiev. The rest went to friends and former employees, save one internal frame backpack and a small leather briefcase. Georgi drove me to the train station and carried the pack down to the platform where the night train for Minsk was boarding. (Ukrainian chivalry does not allow women to carry heavy bags.)

"*Shchastlivo.*" (Have a good one.)

"*Spasibo. Do svidanya.*" (Thank you. Goodbye.)

BELARUS

CHAPTER 2

DOG DAYS IN
AN OPPRESSED COUNTRY

Minsk, Belarus, July 3.

It was "Independence Day" in Belarus, but the capital city was not celebrating its recent break from the Soviet Union. Rather, the occasion marked 55 years of independence from occupation by the "German Fascists" (Nazis.) There were a few banners, and the elderly gents had festooned their drab suit jackets with rows of World War II military medals, but otherwise there were no visible celebrations.

At noon I returned to the Hotel *Svislatch* to check in. Fresh off the train from Kiev, I had stowed my baggage in the administrator's office there early in the morning. A different woman was sitting at the desk.

"Hello, I reserved a single room this morning."

"Oh, my dear, I have no room to give you," she sighed. "Wait a moment."

She was busy registering a group of four Chinese visitors, and there were, as usual, lots of forms to fill out. She had run out of police registration slips and was using a scissors to cut new ones apart from a photocopied sheet. The Chinese group leader counted out stacks and stacks of hyper-inflated 500,000-rouble notes to pay the bill. The desk clerk ran them through her bill-counting machine while her printer labored noisily to prepare receipts, yanking paper from a roll that had to be straightened periodically. Finally, all the machines were silent and she turned to hand work again, carefully tearing the printed receipts apart using a ruler as a guide.

It took half an hour to register the group of four. In the meantime, a parade of previously-registered hotel guests came in and out. Since it was noon, some needed to pay for their rooms for the coming *sutki*[5] (in cash, of course, which meant more spins of the bill-counting machine and more receipts.) Another guest needed to pay cash for the telephone call he has just made from his room. (A large sign posted in the hallway warned that all long distance calls were to be paid for within an hour of the time placed.)

At last it was my turn. I filled out a registration form and pushed it across the counter. The clerk smiled sweetly, sorry that she had kept me waiting.

"My goodness, what *are* you?" she asked, staring at my registration form. It listed a Ukrainian place of residence, British employer and US place of passport issuance.

"I'm an American, but I only need an ordinary room."[6]

"Oh, *that* I have," she said with relief, assigning me a room on the fourth floor "without comforts" (no telephone; toilet and shower down the hall.) I counted out 6 million roubles (about $20) for the two-day stay. It was about ten times the amount a local citizen would have paid for the same room. The desk clerk filled out another set of

---

5. Hotel stays in the former Soviet Union are counted not by the night, but by the *sutki*, or 24-hour period. For hotels, a *sutki* runs from noon to noon. After a guest has paid for a full *sutki*, it is possible to pay for an extra half *sutki*, which allows checkout at midnight instead of noon. This is useful if one is catching an evening train.

6. In Soviet times, many hotels were not supposed to register foreigners as guests because the rooms were not considered presentable enough: the shortcomings of Communism might come to light. At present, it is common for a hotel to have some remodeled rooms that are in significantly better condition than the ordinary rooms. Hotel administrators tend to give these rooms to foreigners, but the rooms may be given to citizens of the former Soviet Union if no foreigners are expected. If I had not offered to take an "ordinary" room, it is possible that other guests (citizens of Belarus) would have been "re-settled" in order to provide me with a remodeled "foreigner's" room. See sidebar *Hotel Registration*, page 26.

forms, then flagged down a young male hotel guest who happened ·
by and pressed him into service to carry my pack across the lobby to
the elevator.

On the fourth floor, I handed my hotel registration card to the
dezhurnaya. She opened her key drawer, pulled out a key on a num-
bered wooden fob and led me down a long winding corridor to my
room. The room was well worn but had pleasant wallpaper, hard-
wood floors and a sink. The wood-framed double casement window
opened onto a sagging fire escape platform. A sheet of metal blocked
the well around the fire escape ladder and there was nothing below
the platform but four stories of thin air.

I found the sheet of official "fire precautions" in the drawer of
the large oak desk. It marked an emergency staircase just around
the corner from my room. I checked it out. The door was tightly
locked, but a sign stated that the key was available from the
dezhurnaya. I picked up the "fire precautions" sheet and wound my
way around the corridor to her desk.

"Do you need something?"

"Yes, this sheet states that my emergency exit is here, yet the
door is locked."

"Oh, I have the key."

"Yes, but what if there is a fire? How will I get out if the key is
here and the stairs are there?"

"There isn't going to be a fire."

"But what if there *is*?"

"If there is, you can use this staircase right here."

"What if this staircase is blocked by the fire?"

"If there is a fire, I will come with the key and open the other
staircase. I will be here all night long."

"How are you going to get to the other staircase if the passage is
blocked by the fire?"

"Don't worry. I will come with the key. Every possible problem
has been anticipated. You will be safe."

The state stores in Minsk were less well-stocked, and the clerks
surlier, than in Kiev. The weather was hot and sticky, and the heat

seemed to concentrate in the airless shops.[7] Most of the space in the meat cases was stuffed with bacon fat in various shapes and permutations. There were fresh slabs, salted slabs, convenient half-kilo plastic containers of melted fat, and large-family sized cellophane-wrapped rolls of chunks and trimmings. The rest of the hog was obviously going elsewhere. Few Western products were on the shelves, and there did not seem to be any private supermarkets.

I took the streetcar out to the botanical garden and walked down a long dusty side street to the Palace of Water Sports for a swim. The Belarussian youth were having as much fun splashing in the outdoor pool as the kids back home — and as much fun practicing civil disobedience. A gap in the fence served as a free entrance and the nearby bushes as a free changing room. I opted for the official entrance, plunking down 130,000 roubles (about 40 cents) for an elaborate system of entrance chits and locker tags that kept a small army employed. The smell of fresh bread wafted through the gym and permeated the shower room; part of the building was used as a bakery.

---

7. Belarus is landlocked. It has a continental climate with some marine influence from the Baltic Sea, which lies to the northwest.

CHAPTER 3

DISASTER IN THE SUBWAY ENTRANCE

In the evening I met up with an American lawyer living in Minsk. We took a stroll before dinner.

"This is where it happened," she said, leading the way into a subway entrance near the riverfront park.

A month earlier, 54 people had been crushed to death on the stairs.

"There was a concert in the park, then a sudden thunderstorm, and people raced in here for cover. Most of the victims were young women who fell or were pushed down these steps. They may have toppled over on their high heels, then the crowd simply continued to surge forward, crushing those inside."

The steps were strewn with fresh flowers. Along the stairs, the walls were scribbled with memorials and pasted with pictures, poems and the names and conditions of 44 people still in the hospital. Many were listed as *byez soznaniya* – unconscious. Friends of the victims were standing around quietly, reading the inscriptions or adding to them. One inscription remembered a man who died while holding his six-year-old son overhead, above the crush. The boy lived.

"One of the embassy guys with a medical background told me it was unusual that there were so few injured in relation to the number who died," my friend continued. "He said that usually in an event like this there is a continuum of less seriously injured, more seriously injured, and dead.[8] He thinks a lot of victims suffocated, and that many more could have been saved if the rescue workers had been trained in CPR."[9]

---

8. It is also possible that the less seriously injured chose not to be treated at the hospital, or otherwise fell outside of the official statistics.

9. See sidebar: *To Protect and Serve*, page 14

To Protect and Serve

The lack of first aid training among public servants was evident in another macabre scene I encountered one fine spring Sunday afternoon on the waterfront promenade in Odessa, Ukraine. While jogging among the blossoming fruit trees, near the sandstone caves in which Jewish families had hidden during World War II, a Berkut special forces police car with lights and siren barreled by on the pedestrian path. Earlier during my run, I had passed a single armed Berkut officer strolling in the tall green grass with several civilians. Half an hour later, as I returned along the same path, one of the civilians lay beside the path bleeding, apparently the victim of an accidental shooting. Several other civilians were propping him up and applying pressure to his fresh wound. The four Berkut officers were not assisting. Rather, they stood near their car, pacing and leaning on the hood, each drawing intensely on the stub of a cigarette.

CHAPTER 4

Do I Have to Smuggle My Own Money?

The American lawyer and I continued on to the *Uzbekistan* restaurant for a couple of plates of steaming *pilaf*.

"Did you have any trouble crossing the border from Ukraine?"

"Nope, a stamp in the passport. That was it."

"They didn't make you fill out a declaration?"

"No."

We had crossed the Ukrainian-Belarussian border in the middle of the night. There had been a parade of border guards and customs agents in and out, but none had offered me a declaration form. Undoubtedly, Western travelers were rare on that new international border.

"How much cash are you carrying?"

I told her.

"Oh, *man*, you're going to lose it. You're only allowed to take $500 out of the country unless you declared it coming in. They'll confiscate it at the Lithuanian border, and they're not going to want to hear any excuses about not receiving a declaration when you crossed into the country. I go to Vilnius a lot, and I won't cross that border without an interpreter. They're pretty aggressive."

"What can I do?"

"Have less than $500 out when you cross the border. Put the rest of your money elsewhere."

It seemed a somewhat risky strategy. We were both engaged in legal reform work, and knew that if our efforts made an impact the results would impinge on some official's comfortable lifestyle. Pragmatically, we knew that we could reduce the chance of bringing trouble on ourselves by following the existing laws – even if illogical and convoluted – to the best of our abilities. My colleague, who lived in one of the most oppressive countries of the former Soviet Union, had even registered her cats.

Professionally, the strategy of smuggling out my money was troubling as well. In the course of my work in Ukraine, it had become apparent to me that democracy would not advance until former Soviet citizens broke the habit of sneaking quietly around their poorly drafted laws and began to confront the rule-makers with demands for legislative change. The situation was undoubtedly worse in Belarus. If I, a privileged Western traveler, could not meet the contradictions head-on, how could those living under the heels of the jackboots be expected to challenge the authorities? A Belarussian lawyer who had been stripped of his law license for defending human rights later told me that Belarus was still a country where bureaucratic caprice made it difficult for troublemakers to obtain permission to travel internationally, and where even children, once they tangled with authorities, were whisked off to prison-like reform institutions, never again to emerge from a controlled life in "the system."

In the end, I decided to conceal my extra money, troubling and risky as it was to hide what I knew customs would be looking for. A customs agent who took my money without due process would be no more than a thief, and I owed no duty to a thief to advertise my assets.

CHAPTER 5

LONG LINES AT THE OPERA HOUSE

Minsk, Belarus, July 4.

It was half an hour before curtain time when I pulled open the heavy wooden door to the Opera House ticket office and got behind the two people in line. I had been hanging out at the circus trying to get tickets, which hadn't panned out.

The woman selling tickets was just slamming the window shut and going off somewhere in search of change. We waited. More people gathered behind me. A young woman sidled toward the ticket window.

"Excuse me, I'm in line," I challenged her.

"Yes, of course," she acknowledged, feet planted.

By the time the ticket lady returned there were twenty people in line. She handed back the change and one of the two people ahead of me walked away with tickets. I was now second in line.

Ignoring me, the young woman who had sidled to the front stuck her head in the ticket window.

"I already have a ticket, but I need one for my child."

Of *course*: a special case. An adequate reason to cut the line. The interloper walked away with a ticket.

The man in front of me bought tickets.

A moment later, the ticket lady leaned out the window. "Sorry folks, I just sold the last tickets to this gentleman. That's it."

No one moved. I planted myself squarely in front of the window. The ticket lady was shuffling papers inside.

A voice came from behind me. "Excuse me, I called about the six tickets."

A woman was breathing over my shoulder. An arm stretched past me and a five-dollar bill flew through the window and disappeared quickly under the counter. Six tickets were handed back. (Good seats were less than a dollar at the black market exchange rate.)

"What's *this*?" I asked loudly, trying to sound shocked. "Tickets are available for *American* money?" [10] It had to be a pretty serious offense in this authoritarian state. Maybe if my presence became inconvenient enough a ticket would appear for me as well. After all, I was first in line.

"I ordered the tickets by telephone."

Ah, reason enough. *Another* special case. The exceptions seemed to be swallowing the rule.

"Is that for the price of the tickets, or for something *else?*" I continued, again a little loudly.

"It's a reservation fee," she said flatly, walking away with her six tickets.

I remained planted in front of the window, guarding the opening a little more closely this time. The ticket lady continued to shuffle papers. Finally she looked up.

"What do *you* want?"

"A ticket." (Why do you think I'm standing here?)

"How many."

"One."

"Oh, *that* I can do." She hand-wrote a ticket and took 130,000 roubles from me.

The other tickets she had sold as I stood near the window had been pre-printed, and I wondered at her ability simply to write up an extra one, but it turned out to be a regular seat on the orchestra level and a mediocre performance.

---

10. See sidebar *American Dollars,* page 19.

American Money

U.S. Dollars are a second currency in many parts of the former Soviet Union. Residents track inflation by measuring the exchange rate of their currency against the dollar, and prices of durable goods are tracked, if not quoted or even paid for, in dollars. Even apartments are frequently bought and sold with American cash. (Closing the sale requires the parties to sit around a large table counting out stacks and stacks of bills.)

Local citizens tend not to deposit their money in banks, where many have lost their entire savings in the past through hyperinflation and bank failures. Rather, they try to turn their extra cash into green dollars and hide the money in their apartments. Small money-changing booths on sidewalks and in shops, staffed by live persons, serve as the functional equivalent of automatic teller machines, allowing dollars to be reconverted to local currency when needed for shopping. In Russia a passport is officially required to change money, and exchange booth hours tend to be similar to banking hours. In Ukraine, these booths are open much longer hours, and most change money on a no-questions-asked basis, scrutinizing only the quality of the bills offered. Posters issued by the United States Treasury, detailing identifying features of legitimate U.S. currency, are tacked on the walls of many booths as a means of educating customers about counterfeits. American cash bearing a series number before 1992 is virtually impossible to exchange.

In Ukraine, private money changing also occurs directly between shoppers and small entrepreneurs (usually middle-aged women bundled against the cold in winter) who stroll in small groups in shopping districts, quietly advertising their profession as money-changers by their large black purses, worn on a leather strap over the neck and one shoulder.

CHAPTER 6

THE TRAIN TO GRODNO

Minsk, Belarus, July 5, 11:00 p.m.

The last bit of light was leaving the summer sky as the electric train pulled into the station and made ready for boarding. An energetic young *provodnitsa* stepped out of the car and, using a lunchbox-sized searchlight (the kind with a big square box for the battery hanging down below the handle), checked my ticket and let me board.

It was a *kupé* train car, part of the former Soviet rolling stock. It looked like every other *kupé* from Odessa to Vladivostok. There was a long narrow corridor along one side of the car and a row of compartments with heavy metal sliding doors along the other side. A wool runner rug ran the length of the corridor, and a continuous length of linen toweling lay atop the runner rug to absorb the wear and tear and dirt of heavy foot traffic. Fold-down jumpseats were spaced beneath the windows along the corridor, but anyone sitting in one would have to pop up and down constantly to let fellow travelers by. There was a washroom at each end of the car, locked during the station stop. Next to one washroom was the *provodnitsa's* compartment, and in the corridor outside her compartment was a coal-fired *samovar*, continuously boiling water for tea. It was the *provodnitsa's* job periodically to shove grimy black chunks of coal into the bottom of the *samovar* from an iron bucket sitting on the floor below.

I found the four-bed compartment noted on my ticket. The heavy door slid open smoothly on its track and latched tightly from the inside.[11] Inside were two sets of bunk beds with a small

---

11. See sidebar *Train Safety,* page 22.

table between them, by the window. There was a large shiny mirror on the inside of the door. Four pillows and four blankets were rolled up inside four heavy cotton mattresses, ready for nighttime use. There was room for luggage both in an open space on the floor under the lower bunks and in a metal well reachable by lifting up the bottom bunk on a hinge. More luggage could be placed in a hollow above the compartment's sliding door.

I shoved my bags on the top bunk. Surprisingly, neither of the two men in the compartment got up to help. Perhaps Belarussian chivalry was a little different from Ukrainian.

At 11:23 p.m., just like clockwork, the train began to move. The compartment was a stuffy 40 degrees Celsius (104 Fahrenheit) and the wood-framed window was stuck open just a crack. The two men worked and worked to free it. Finally the rain-swollen sash moved, the window slid open 18 inches, and the sweet cool night air poured in.

Oops! That was not what they wanted. The men worked and worked until the sash moved again and the window was sealed tightly. The Belarussians, it seemed, like the Ukrainians, had an aversion to night drafts. I looked around for another compartment I might switch to, but everywhere folks were already bedding down in the fresh clean sheets rented from the *provodnitsa* and there were no empty spaces.

Train Safety

I traveled about twelve thousand miles alone on post-Soviet trains without a problem, including two dozen overnight trips. But spending the night on the train can be dangerous. In separate incidents, three close colleagues were drugged and robbed on trains in the former East Bloc during the late 1990's. One, a Ukrainian woman travelling with a friend, fell into a deep sleep on a Ukrainian train after accepting a glass of champagne from a young man who brought an already-opened bottle to her compartment, claiming that he was celebrating the birth of a new baby. Another, a British ex-patriate sleeping alone in a First Class compartment on a Ukrainian train, awoke in the morning from a very deep sleep to discover that seven thousand dollars he was carrying to a provincial city to meet payroll for his employees had been stolen. The money had been in a suitcase in the metal well underneath his bunk, which was reachable only by lifting him and his bedding off the bunk as he slept. He, too, had somehow been drugged. After a morning of feeling dizzy he collapsed and spent three days in the hospital, unable to move his limbs. A third colleague, an American woman of Polish descent, was robbed after being gassed at night along with her mother and sister in their train compartment while travelling through Poland. Similar incidents have occurred in Russia.

While these incidents are unnerving and can be truly hazardous, they must be considered in context: train travel – not air or highway travel – is the most popular means of inter-city transit in the former Soviet Union, and many, many people reach their destinations safely.

For safety, I chose to travel in four-bed kupés rather than the two-bed First Class lux compartments. While this afforded less privacy, it allowed me to appear less ostentatious and also reduced the chance of being alone with one stranger inside a locked compartment. (Train employees have socket-wrench like "keys" which can open locked compartments from the outside. Border guards and other outsiders undoubtedly gain access to such "keys" as well.) In addition, I never wore jewelry or showed any other valuables while on the train. Upon boarding a train in the evening for an overnight trip, I made a point of not speaking, but simply acting tired, making up my bed and going to sleep. In this way, I revealed nothing about myself before the most dangerous part of the trip. Until morning, my fellow travelers could be allowed to think that I had friends sleeping in the compartment next door. Most importantly, by keeping my mouth shut, no one would hear my foreign accent and I could pass as a native making a short trip to visit relatives (for which I would ostensibly need to carry little money.) Embarrassingly, I was so successful at portraying this image that one man, thinking me destitute, bought me a glass of tea.

Sometimes the provodnitsas would blow my cover. They always check passports against the passport number on the passenger's ticket to prevent the fraudulent use of discount tickets by non-military, non-invalids, etc. Thus, they are aware when they have a foreigner on board.

The Belarussian Countryside, July 6, 6:20 a.m.

The train slowed suddenly. I awoke from a deep sleep to a loud one-word greeting from the *provodnitsa*.

"Grodno!"

It turned out to be an hour before arrival time, but we were expected to rise, make our beds, and deliver the sheets and pillowcases to the *provodnitsa* for inventory. By the time I emerged from the compartment, a number of people were already lined up by the WC at the end of the hall, linen towels (issued by the *provodnitsa*) slung around their necks; sandwich bags with a ration of pink toilet paper (also officially issued) in their hands.

The train was travelling through grain and potato fields. A windbreak of trees separated the large collective and state farm fields from a narrow strip of private plots planted along the train tracks. Here and there a tethered goat or cow grazed in the woodland strip.

CHAPTER 7

THE CITY BUS

Grodno, Belarus, July 6, 7:20 a.m.

The train pulled into Grodno right on time. Bus Number 15 was standing at the turnaround in front of the station, full, ready to leave. The nearby ticket booth was closed. I squeezed in the front door of the bus and tendered 6,000 roubles to the driver for a ticket.

"I can't sell you one," grunted the driver, a slight, surly fellow. "Buy one from another passenger." Meanwhile, he continued to sell handfuls of tickets to other passengers.

It turned out that tickets were sold only in strips of five. Unfortunately for the driver, the tickets were *printed* in unperforated strips of *six*. At each stoplight, the driver took out a small, dull, child's scissors and snipped one ticket off the end of each strip. He collected the "singles" in a crack in the dashboard until he had five, then sold them as a strip.

I purchased a strip of five. The driver stuffed my 30,000 roubles into a portfolio overflowing with tattered, high-numbered bills. Several bills fluttered to the floor under the gas pedal. He stooped to collect them, muttering.

The markings on the bus showed that it had had a long journey to reach Grodno. The windshield was printed with maintenance instructions from a German municipality; a sign stenciled on the door in Czech warned not to lean against the door while the bus was travelling. No doubt the driver had as many frustrations to deal with under the hood as with the tickets.

Chapter 8

Hotel Belarus

At the front desk of the Hotel Belarus, a small handwritten sign was taped up: "No hot water from July 5 through July 25." No great loss. It was only 8:00 a.m. and already sweltering.

"Do you have any single rooms?"

"No."

"Will you have any after twelve o'clock?"

"Oh, probably. There's a good chance," said the administrator absent-mindedly, shuffling papers and looking off somewhere else.

"In the meantime do you have a baggage room?"

My accent caught her attention. She focussed on me.

"Where are you from?"

I handed over my American passport.

She squinted at it, unable to read the English letters in my name. Finally she flipped to the page with the Belarussian visa, written in Cyrillic, and began writing in her register.

"I can give you a room now," she said.[12] "Come back later for your passport."[13]

---

12. As a western foreigner I was automatically given preferential treatment.

13. See sidebar *Hotel Registration,* page 26.

Hotel Registration

Most former Soviet hotels have both an administrator and a cashier at the front desk. The administrator is the one to approach even if there is a line of people waiting for her attention and the cashier is doing nothing. To register, the guest must fill out a registration form and present a passport and, in the case of a foreigner, a visa. Foreigners are often excused from filling out the registration form. This appears to stem partly from the fact that the registration forms are often written only in Russian, in which case it is easier for the administrator to simply take the guest's passport and extract the necessary information; and in part from the fact that many hotel registration forms contain a statement at the bottom which the (Russian-speaking) guest is required to sign, agreeing to vacate the room in the event that a foreigner arrives later and needs a room.

The administrator records the guest's name and passport information in her log, stamps the visa with the hotel's registration stamp and notes the dates of arrival and departure. An administrator will sometimes tell you to come back later to retrieve your passport. This usually happens if a lot of guests have arrived during a short space of time, in order to allow the administrator to catch up on the paperwork without keeping you waiting. If you politely tell the administrator that you don't mind waiting, you can usually retrieve your passport and visa within a few minutes, which is well worth the peace of mind, as passports can get misplaced.

Payment usually must be made in cash. Credit cards are catching on in the more progressive-minded and upscale places, but should not be relied on exclusively as a means of payment. A credit card sticker posted at the hotel does not necessarily mean that you can pay for a room with a credit card. It may be an advertisement offering cash advances from a money exchange service which rents space in the hotel but keeps banker's hours; or it may be that car rental can be paid for with a credit card but room rental cannot. In addition, credit cards sometimes do not pass electronic approval for reasons having nothing to do with the validity of the card. The quality of the telephone line to the verification point may be poor, or the proprietor may simply prefer to be paid in cash, which is easier to receive off the books and thus escape notice of the tax inspector. (This seems to be more of a problem in restaurants than hotels.)

If credit cards are not accepted (or if yours is not) and you have not exchanged enough money to pay in cash, you can sometimes agree to pay for the room later. Hotels will not normally accept payment in hard currency. It is also quite normal to pay for the room for only one sutki, or 24-hour period, at a time. This is particularly a good idea if you have arrived in a small town on a weekend, when currency exchange booths may not be open.

After payment is made, the hotel administrator or cashier will hand back a receipt, a hotel guest card showing the room number and the dates of residence, and, if breakfast is included, a chit (talon) to give to the waiter or waitress. Sometimes the key is handed out at the front desk, but in more traditional hotels it will be handed out by the dezhurnaya on the floor where the guest is registered. Often, the dezhurnaya will demand to keep the guest's receipt until departure. This seems to be viewed as a sort of collateral to help ensure payment of telephone bills and the like. Once in a while a dezhurnaya will demand that the key be left with her each time the guest leaves the floor. This is not necessarily a sign of obstinacy; it could be that there is only one key in existence and she is terrified that the guest will lose it.

Regardless of whether you keep the key in your possession or leave it with the dezhurnaya, it is important to keep the hotel card with you at all times, as you may need to show it upon returning to the hotel to get past the security guards.

I took the creaking elevator to the fourth floor, where a sweet elderly *dezhurnaya* wrote my name in the roster and handed me a room key.

"Is there a place to change money downstairs?"

She and her co-worker exchanged glances. "Uh, yes."

I went to my room. It was the best hotel in town; the foreigner's price was about $7 a night. The TV worked on two channels. The bathroom was done in typical Soviet style,[14] with a small strip of mirror mounted at shoulder height, so that anyone over 4'10" had to stoop to see themselves. There was no shower stall – just a shower nozzle mounted on one wall, directly over the wavy tile floor. The toilet seat was hand cut from varnished plywood.

There was a knock at the door. It was the elderly *dezhurnaya*. She would be glad to change money for me; I did not need to go downstairs. She could give me a better rate too: 400,000 roubles to the dollar instead of the 300,000 offered at official booths. She was expecting a new grandchild, and needed hard currency to buy a gift.

I gave her a crisp new $20.

She held it up. "I'm not even sure what these are supposed to look like."

I showed her the watermark of Andrew Jackson and the red and blue threads in the paper. She thanked me and left.

At the top floor *bufet* the tables were covered with pretty pink cotton tablecloths. Sprigs of fresh incense cedar were stuck in flower vases on each table. Several guests were breakfasting on grayish wieners, slices of tomato and cheese. Unappetizing plates of pre-fried food sat behind a glass case, waiting to be re-heated upon a guest's request.

I ordered some tea and asked for a bottle of the apple juice on display on the shelf behind the counter. The bottle was as warm as the day.

"Do you have a cold one?"

"No."

---

14. See sidebar *Hot and Cold Water,* page 29.

I strolled around town, seemingly the only tourist. The café in the park was filled with animated young people dining on ice cream, beer, shredded cabbage with large dollops of cream, and vodka. The vodka was sold in round carafes by the 100 ml, filled with a measuring beaker by the counter lady.

The smaller children in town had taken refuge from the heat at FOK, a 50-meter indoor pool on Gorky Street. A swarm of kids was admitted and chased out each hour by a staff of tired large-sized women who, between shifts of teeming youngsters, alternated mopping the slick floor and their brows.

Early the next morning there was a knock at my hotel room door.
"Who is it?"
"It's the *dezhurnaya*. Let me in."
"But I'm not dressed yet."
"Throw something on. I need to take furniture out of your room."
I let her in.

"Sorry to bother you, but I need the *tumbochka*." She was already moving the things I had laid out on it. "We've been waiting for a month for the truck to arrive to take these away, and it has finally shown up unexpectedly." She hoisted away a small wooden cupboard and disappeared.

Hot and Cold Water

Soviet-style hot and cold water taps are the reverse of Western ones. (Hot is on the right.) Recently remodeled bathrooms often follow the Western custom of placing the hot water on the left. Sometimes it is difficult to guess which custom is being followed, and difficult to tell whether the water isn't getting hot because you have the wrong faucet on or because the hot water is not working.

CHAPTER 9

NIGHTMARE AT CUSTOMS

Grodno, Belarus, July 7.

It was time to board the train to Vilnius, Lithuania.

Grodno, on the border with both Poland and Lithuania, had an elaborate customs hall in the train station with more agents on duty than the 'Arrivals' terminal at Heathrow Airport. All passengers bound for international trains needed to pass through it prior to boarding.

I retrieved my pack from the left luggage room in the basement, concealed my extra cash on my person (on the advice of my friend in Minsk), made my way through a gauntlet of Belarussian citizens hoping I was going to Poland and would carry letters across for them,[15] and entered the iron-barred entrance chute. It was 25 minutes before train time.

Inside the sterile, brightly-lit, high-ceilinged customs hall were two rows of stainless steel counters. I was directed to the "women's" side, on the right, and met by a well-coifed, bleached blond customs lady with too much lipstick. She had obviously eaten well since the acquisition of her uniform, which was now under some stress to accommodate her ample figure.

---

15. It is unlikely that the destitute Belarussians plying me with envelopes were sending their hyper-inflated money to friends in Poland. Most likely, the envelopes contained personal correspondence; perhaps pleas for money to relatives abroad, or news about their families that they did not want to risk sharing with a nosy customs official, or simply did not trust would be delivered if placed in the normal postal system (see sidebar *Postal Service*, page 97.) But it is also possible that the envelopes contained contraband that they hoped to dupe an innocent stranger into carrying across the border for them.

"Declaration, please."

"I don't have one. They did not hand out any forms on the train from Kiev."

She looked skeptical, but continued breezily with one eye on the clock.

"Show me your money."

I handed her what was in my wallet: U.S. dollars, a few German marks, traveler's checks. Each currency had to be noted separately on the declaration form. I watched, pen in hand, as she counted each stack, dutifully writing the total amount of each currency on the form. I was beginning to wonder whether it had been such a hot idea to put the rest of my money away, but there was no graceful way to retrieve it now.

"Fill out the rest of this declaration," she ordered, hurriedly directing me from one blank to the next. "Write '*nyet*' here, '*nyet,*' '*nyet,*' '*nyet…*'"

"Just a moment. I haven't had time to read the questions," I protested.

"You aren't carrying any narcotics, are you?"

"No."

"Then hurry up. Sign it here." She was already reaching for a hand-held metal detector.

My hand shook wildly as I signed. (Had she noticed?)

Another passenger was approaching the counter.

"Men have to go to *that* side." She redirected him to the opposite stainless steel counter, using the metal detector as a pointer. Apparently a body search was next.

My heart beat faster. I broke into a sweat, and the crisp, concealed cash against my body seemed to take on a life of its own: rustling, prickling, silently shouting its presence. In spite of the bright lights, the room seemed to be going dark as the blood rushed from my head.

"Now, do you have any money you haven't told me about yet?" the bright red lips were saying, as if reading my mind.

That was a direct question and there was no ducking it. The trap was set. If I said "no" I might get away with it. I needed that cash. Where I was headed there would be many times when cash or the kindness of strangers would be the only means of survival. But it was a slippery slope. I would be a hypocrite to the rule of law which I had worked so hard to instill in Ukraine. And if she found it, I would certainly lose it and might be arrested, caught in a tangled web of my own weaving.

If I said "yes" there would be trouble for sure, but perhaps it would not be as difficult to smooth over. At this juncture my disclosure would still be voluntary, and at bottom I would be on the right side of the law, such as it was.

I had only a split second to respond.

"Why yes. But I don't want to pull it out *here*. Dangerous people ride the train."

Dark thunderclouds rolled in and blotted out her sunny disposition. "WHAT??? You have money that you didn't TELL me about??" Her tone of voice suggested that I had committed the crime of the century. At the least, I had flouted her authority. Clearly, I should now be redirected to a train bound for Siberia. Many, perhaps thousands, had undoubtedly passed through this very station on their way to prison camps, their lives changed forever on similarly flimsy pretexts.

"I'm telling you about it now." My mouth felt like it was filled with cotton. "Perhaps you'd like me to add it to the declaration. Where is it?"

I looked around, but the stainless steel counter, gleaming under the intense mercury vapor lights, was bare. She wasn't about to give the declaration back. The object of this exercise was not disclosure but entrapment, and I was captured meat.

She hollered across the cavernous hall for her supervisor.

A distant voice responded. Her supervisor was busy.

No matter, she would make good use of the time.

"Open these bags!" she ordered. It was fifteen minutes to train departure time.

I undid the tiny padlocks and pulled the zippers.

She rummaged, more interested in turning the pages of each book and notebook (hoping, no doubt, that big green bills would flutter out) than in examining the large stockpile of just-in-case medicines

I was carrying for my three-month tour through the wilderness of the former Worker's Paradise.

It was five minutes to train time. At last her supervisor was available. But that alone was not enough. Every customs lady on duty, seven or eight in all, reported to the steel counter. Surrounded by this peroxided and bright-lipsticked detachment in their gray-blue uniforms and uncomfortable Soviet-made high heels, I was escorted past smoked glass windows, around a corner, down a corridor and into a back room. I was no doubt a curiosity in a land devoid of tourists, and everyone needed a story to tell when she went home to her dingy apartment that evening. My luggage, sitting alone on the stainless steel counter back in the main customs hall, was the least of my concerns at the moment.

The back room seemed to be the customs ladies' cloak room. There was a mirror on one wall, and a pile of purses on a wooden bench.

I halted in the middle of the room and spun around, facing them all. I took a deep breath. It was time to play the best cards up my sleeve.

"First of all, here is my identification from the embassy in Kiev." I handed over two photo ID cards. "Second, here is the rest of my money." I pulled out a stack of bills, probably disappointingly thin to those who had envisioned a great bust.

The delivery had come off well. By boldly admitting to the extra currency, I had thrown them for a loop, for it was not the usual practice among travelers in this part of the world. The greedy customs agents could not play out the time-honored scenario of catching the traveler in a bald lie, then reducing their prey to a groveling basket case, eager to give any amount of money simply to be released. Further, in their minds, anyone who would be so audacious as to admit they were carrying more than the allowed amount must indeed have the power to do so. (Power and legal right being two very different things.)

Now the quandary was theirs: entrapment was not intended to be practiced against well-connected people. Such people are above the law, and causing them difficulties can backfire badly on an ordinary rank-and-file customs agent. It simply wasn't worth risking a career over.[16] In addition, I sensed that I had been able to convey enough warmth that they had taken a liking to me.

They escorted me back to the main hall. They seemed inclined to release me, but there was a problem: they did not have the authority to do so under the circumstances. The decision would have to be made by the head of the customs station.

"Give me your passport and ID cards," she ordered. "Stand over here with this guard."

One of the ladies ran the papers upstairs. The two-story tall customs hall, I now noticed, was built in a fishbowl fashion, with a mezzanine level overlooking the search-and-interrogation counters. The mezzanine walls were entirely of glass, covered by drawn venetian blinds. The director's office was obviously behind one of the blinds.

The customs ladies watched the blinds intently, glancing at the clock from time to time. Hopefully, the director was at his desk, not on the telephone, and not with buddies who did not like to be interrupted. It was past train departure time.

"Has the train left?"

"No, we're holding it for you. This is an *international* train, you know." She emphasized the gravity of the delay. "Next time, tell us about all of your currency right away." Though she was still scolding, she had turned back into a human being.

I was still holding my breath. One of the ID cards I had given her was expired, and it wasn't a real get-out-of-jail-free card anyway. Besides, there was no assurance the Belarussian authorities would pay any heed even to the best paperwork. A chunk of the local diplomatic community had found itself without utilities the year before, when Belarussian President Lukashenko had taken a liking to their compound and had not so subtly encouraged them to move out.

---

16. Other low-level law enforcement employees have to be careful as well. In some former Soviet countries, including Russia and Ukraine, important people are issued special license plates. Traffic police are able to discern at a glance what ministry a person works for and, depending on the pecking order, will avoid stopping the vehicles of powerful people who have violated traffic laws.

The customs ladies continued to watch the venetian blinds for a sign. Finally, it came: a thumbs up. No *protokol* was to be drawn up and I was to be released.

"Here, quick, change your declaration to add the rest of the money to it." Magically, the long-hidden declaration reappeared.

"I don't remember the amount."

"*I* do. Don't bother counting it again." She dictated the amount to me. "There, now go."

"I need my passport back."

"It's coming. You just stand here. The guard will escort you to the train."

I watched as the little blue book that separated me from all of them was carried down to the end of the customs hall by a bear of a man in a customs agent's uniform and held hostage in a small glass booth. Someone was punching at a computer. The minutes ticked by.

Finally the officer brought it back to me. "Here, get on the train. But your problems are not over yet. You don't have a visa, so you're likely to get sent back from the border."

"Of *course* I have a visa – here it is." I pointed to the large stiff Belarussian sticker firmly clamped over an entire page of my passport. Goodness, how could I have gotten this far without one?

"No, we mean a *Lithuanian* visa."

"I don't *need* one of those – I'm an American," I called over my shoulder as the young guard led me away.

It must have really fried him. The pristine sandy beaches of the former Soviet colonies on the Baltic were now available to his kin on an 'invitation only' basis.

"*Harrumph*, we'll see."

The guard I was assigned to marched me to the nearest train car. The train began to move the moment I stepped on. "Make sure she gets to the right car," the guard barked at the *provodnik*.

I found the chair car going to Vilnius, completely empty, with the wind blowing freely through wide-open windows. The air was cool and sweet.

PART 11

THE BALTICS

LITHUANIA

CHAPTER 1

THE PATRIOTIC SCHOOLTEACHER

Vilnius, Lithuania, July 7.

The hallway of Irena's apartment was graced with the horns and antlers of stately proud creatures that, like many of the *Partisani* of the 1940's and early 50's, fell to gunshots in the Lithuanian forests.

Irena was a cheery and outgoing retired schoolteacher. "My pension is $18 a month. I'm lucky to have a two-room[17] apartment, because the second room can be let out for money to keep my grandchildren in candy."

Irena had bought her Soviet-issued apartment from the government ten years earlier, when it first became possible, by making payments to the state housing authority. She still paid utilities. Gas and electricity were separately metered.

"We lived well during Soviet times. Electricity was cheap. Everything is more expensive now. They keep telling us: 'Well, it's even more expensive in the West.' But of course the salaries are higher in the West as well. Now we're allowed to travel, but we have no money to travel."

"Nonetheless," she continued, "I would *never* go back to the old

---

17. Hallways, kitchens and bathrooms are not included in the room count. Most 'rooms' serve multiple purposes: sleeping, dining, watching television, receiving friends, etc.

system. Yes, we had a good standard of living then, but now we have something for our souls: *freedom.*" She clasped her hands. "I'm *so* proud."

I mentioned my visit to the former KGB prison in the basement of a city building in Vilnius, now a museum. It had cells as small as telephone booths and peepholes everywhere.

"We don't need that museum," she retorted. "The whole thing should be bulldozed. The only museum we need is an empty square with a plaque saying 'NEVER AGAIN.' One third of the Lithuanian people were killed or sent to Siberia by the Communists.[18] My brother was one of them. There was a celebration on the anniversary of Lenin's death. My brother had finished a bottle of wine and announced: '...and if *Stalin* dies, I'll drink *two* bottles.' *TEN YEARS* they gave him for saying that!" She shook her fist. "We only found out where he was through a note he dropped on the railroad tracks, addressed to us. Some brave, anonymous person got it to us. At first we could not even send him any packages. After Stalin died things got a little better. My brother came back with no teeth; there had been some kind of epidemic in the camp."

We talked about the newly developing Lithuanian economy.

"We have food products coming out of our ears. Milk especially. Exporting it is difficult, though. The Western Europeans already have their own. The Belarussians need it, but they already owe us a ton of money."

"What are the prospects for getting the debt paid?"

"The Belarussians make pretty good tractors. They could send us some. We don't have a tractor factory of our own."

Irena's bathroom was newly remodeled. It turned out that her daughter, an interior designer, had played a hand in it. Her daughter apparently did not suffer from the same economic hardships as Irena — she would be jetting off to Tunisia for vacation over the summer.

---

18. Other sources estimate that from 120,000 to 300,000 citizens of this tiny country were lost. There are about 3 million ethnic Lithuanians in the country today.

LATVIA

CHAPTER 2

THE FRIGHTENED PENSIONER

Riga, Latvia, July 14, 10:00 p.m.

The sun was an orange globe over the grainfields as the Volvo bus breezed along the smooth road and into the city limits. I was to spend the night with Anna, a woman I had never met, who supplemented her pension by renting out her second room.

Anna had an apartment on the main boulevard. I hiked up the dark stairs to the second floor, located the flat number with a flashlight, and pressed the bell. A quavering voice came from the other side of the door. I described who I was. From inside came the sounds of the unbolting of many locks; then the door creaked open. An elderly woman motioned me in, obviously terrified of letting a stranger into her home, but needing the $15 I was to pay her for the night so badly that she had to take the chance.

I put my pack down and pointed to myself. "English, *Deutsch, Russkii.*"

"Latvian," she said firmly, pointing to herself.

I didn't believe her. No one who has lived through half a century of Russian occupation completely avoids learning the language, yet I respected her decision not to speak it. A few minutes later, after sign language to explain the quirks of various faucets and locks around the apartment became difficult, she admitted that she spoke a little German; then Russian words started coming through as well.

40

She showed me the bathroom. There was no sink; the toothbrushes and mirror were hung over the tub, which gurgled its used contents into a square open drain in the cement floor. Enamel washing basins were stacked in a corner, on top of the portable cylinder of a semi-automatic wash machine. The simple bathroom had one luxury item found in many Soviet-built apartments: a heated towel rack. That is, the pipes of the central hot water system wound around into two thicker, shoulder-height horizontal pipes just long enough for a towel, or perfect for drying a few pairs of socks washed in one of the enamel basins. However, since the "heating season" was long past, the pipes would be cold until fall.

My bedroom was also the living room/dining room. There was a long wooden hutch along the far wall, filled with elegant glassware and a row of books, neatly lined up but seemingly unread. The rotary-dial telephone was covered with a small tapestry cloth, perhaps against potential dust; perhaps to deter overnight guests from unauthorized use.

I awoke early the next morning to a stern rap at the door. The sun was already streaming in and Anna stood in the doorway in her going-to-market clothes.

"I need forty-five dollars from you for three nights' lodging." She was all business. No doubt a fee was owed to the broker who had organized my stay, and it would be a financial disaster for her if I were to slip away while she was out at the market. Perhaps she was hungry, as well. It is possible that she had no money when I arrived.

I roused myself and found some American cash for her.

41

CHAPTER 3

THE NOT-QUITE-
POST-SOVIET WAITER

Smaragd's Café, Old Town Riga, Latvia, July 15.

The atmosphere was silken. The subdued lighting subtly enhanced the wood and raspberry interior. The distinguished looking, white-jacketed waiter fetched a menu in English[19] while I surreptitiously scrabbled in the polished wainscoting for an electric socket for my laptop.

Moments later the magic atmosphere was broken when an ancient Soviet-built truck chugged by the open doorway, belching a choking blue diesel plume into the café.

The waiter returned with a hearty bowl of *khapach* and ordered me to put my computer away. "No business! Your soup will get cold."

A piano player appeared and the silken atmosphere returned.

The bill arrived. It was twice the sum of the items I had ordered, with separate charges added for the bread, the service and the music. No complaints there; all three had been superb. But there was one item I felt compelled to challenge.

"You've charged me three times as much for the mineral water as the price on the menu."

"I know. The price went up. We tried to change it on all the menus, but apparently we forgot one. Unfortunately it was the menu

---

19. Menus, signs and other written materials in the Baltics are now in the local language rather than in Russian, and bookstores offer general pleasure reading books to local citizens in many Western European languages. Older Baltic citizens, such as the waiter, usually speak Russian as well as their native language. Young people are flocking to learn English. Those involved in tourism in the Baltics often have German speakers on staff as well.

you got. I'm awfully sorry — it was our mistake."

He stood expectantly.

"Then you can correct it."

He stood still, looking puzzled. Finally my meaning dawned: "Oh, yes, of course!" He unplanted his feet and brought back a revised bill.

CHAPTER 4

THE COUNTRY HOUSE

Riga, Latvia, July 17, 4:00 p.m.

I stood under the clock tower of the Riga train station at the appointed hour. A sixty-ish woman in a white eyelet blouse approached me shyly, made eye contact, and gingerly asked my name. Yes, it was my next hostess, Velta. She led me to a red Ford Escort where her husband Evald was waiting with two small grandsons, and we began the three-hour journey to their house in the country near Jekabpils, in Eastern Latvia.

The trip turned into a history and economics lesson. The Ford Escort was a used German-built model acquired last year to replace the couple's Soviet-built *Zhiguli*. It was bought through a trader who specialized in bringing in used cars from Germany. [20] The couple had driven to Riga earlier in the day to drop their daughter off at the ferry port for the return trip to her job in Oslo, Norway where she could earn a higher salary than in Latvia.

We left the city behind, travelling inland along the River Daugava.

"This was the front line between the Germans and the Russians in World War I. The river was one of the reasons why the Russians were always interested in controlling the Baltics. Before the railway and highway were built, this river was a major trade route because the Daugava is connected with the Volga and the Dnieper near

---

20. Used cars and trucks from western Europe (particularly Germany) and Japan are preferred by many former Soviet drivers over new Russian-built cars.

Smolensk.[21] The river connections through Saint Petersburg are not nearly as good."

We continued upstream past three hydroelectric power stations. Ugly cement-block apartment buildings lined the road near the dams.

"The construction workers lived here while building the power station. Stalin deported our people to Siberia[22] and brought in Russians to fill the labor deficit."

We passed a sugar refinery – now closed. "It used to process locally-grown sugar beets and, during the off season, raw cane imported from Cuba."

Dairy barns from now-defunct collective farms also stood empty along the road.

Forests, small farmsteads and green meadows with golden haystacks appeared, then more ugly apartment blocks.

"Five major factories were built in this area; the apartments were built for the workers. Four of the plants have now closed; only the glass factory is still working."

"And the Russian workers?"

"They're still here. They can become Latvian citizens by taking a

Network of Rivers

The Volga River flows through southern Russia and empties into the Caspian Sea just below Astrakhan; the Dnieper River flows through Ukraine and empties into the Black Sea near Odessa. Other navigable waterways connect with Saint Petersburg and with Lake Onega near Petrozavodsk, forming an extensive inland water transportation network. The water level in the Daugava River, with its many dams, is nearly low enough to wade across now, making navigation virtually impossible.

21. See sidebar *Network of Rivers*.

22. There are estimates that at least 57,000 Latvians were deported. Today there are about 1.3 million ethnic Latvians living in the country.

three-part test, which includes Latvian history and language. Those who do not pass the test get a non-citizen's passport. They can travel but they cannot vote. Some of the Russians are angry about it. They say things like: 'We should have sent even more of you to Siberia.'"

Jekabpils, Latvia, July 17.

We stopped for supper at a roadside café outside of town and washed up at the sink in the corner of the dining room before ordering.[23] The menu was brief but the food hearty and homemade. Before the war, Evald explained, the main street of this town along the Daugava River had been filled with dozens of tiny shops. The invading Nazis had evicted all the Jewish shopkeepers, and they had not returned.

Several kilometers beyond the town we turned in at a small house on the riverbank with an enormous garden. Velta asked me to stay inside the house while the couple's ferocious dog was allowed a few minutes of exercise. Large trucks lumbered noisily past on the two-lane highway.

---

23. In many parts of the former Soviet Union, hand-washing before sitting down to a meal is as much of a ritual as giving toasts.

CHAPTER 5

SUNDAY IN THE COUNTRY

Jekabpils, Latvia, July 18.

In Velta and Ewald's garden, the red currants were ripe. Evald and I picked a couple of large bowls full to make *kompot*. Velta uprooted a few carrots for Sunday dinner's soup before calling us in to a breakfast of boiled eggs, slices of sausage, cheese, cucumbers, pickles and tomatoes, and a bowl of potato salad decorated with spikes of green onion and a sprig of blooming dill from the garden. There was a mug of boiled milk fresh from the neighbor's cow.

"We had our own cow for the first five years after we retired. It was too much work. We were always scrabbling around for hay for it, which we had to gather by hand."

Next came a mushroom-hunting expedition in the woods across the road. Too dry. We found a few, but tossed them aside; small hungry creatures, like worms in apples, had burrowed through the delicious stems. The weather also had been too dry for wild berries.

"These ten hectares[24] of forest are ours again. They belonged to my grandfather before the German and Soviet occupations. In winter we cut our Christmas tree here, and last year a big pine tree fell here. We sawed it up for wood to heat the house."

Onward over moguled dirt roads to a glacially-formed lake for a swim. We changed in the woods. A turnoff from the dirt road led straight into the lake, but a huge pile of sand had been dumped fifty feet short of the water, blocking vehicle traffic.

"This sandpile is a wonderful thing," said Velta. "Before, people used to drive straight into the lake and wash their cars there."

---

24. A hectare is equivalent to about 2.5 acres.

ESTONIA

CHAPTER 6

OPTIMISTIC YOUTH

Tallinn, Estonia, July 21.

I met up with Tula and Pekka and we went out for a dinner of wild boar in the Old Town. Later, we walked around the parapets of the castle in the late summer evening light and finished the night at an airy new second-floor café overlooking the square.

"The best way to reach me is on my mobile phone," said Pekka. "We just moved out of my mother's house."

The Little Nation That Can

Estonia, a tiny country on the Baltic coast near Finland, was one of the first to declare independence from the Soviet Union, in August 1991, sealing the event with a spontaneous songfest on the water's edge. Among the former East Bloc countries, it is a first-round candidate to join the European Union. Though often lumped together with Latvia and Lithuania as one of the three "Baltic States," Estonians are re-lated by similar language to Finns, and feel a close kinship with the Finns. Their language is not related to Latvian or Lithuanian. Reli-gious Estonians tend to be Lutheran.

Border controls among the Baltic countries, and between Estonia and Finland, are much lighter than border controls in the Slavic coun-tries of the former Soviet Union.

Though they were both several years out of the university, their current living quarters were definitely student style.

"Having several generations under one roof is not typical for Estonians, who value privacy more than camaraderie. Mom has a huge place, but we felt like we didn't have our own lives. She always wanted to do things with us."

We sat cross-legged on the floor to look at pictures of a recent mountain-climbing expedition in the Alps. Tula made a cup of *kama* for me to try. It was an ancient Estonian specialty consisting of grain powder stirred into *kefir*.

"How do Estonians characterize themselves in relation to their European neighbors?"

"We are not as likely to be forward in expressing our viewpoint. Rather, we're likely to listen first and keep our opinions to ourselves. It's probably a survival instinct. Germans, for example, are a large power; Estonians are a small group. Thus, Germans can afford to be more outspoken and demanding. For the same reason, Estonians do not wear their religion on their sleeves. One's beliefs are a private thing."

"Ten thousand Estonians were sent to Siberia during the Stalin years. That's a huge number in light of our small population.[25] But I'm not one of those people who refuses to have anything to do with the Russians," Pekka continued. "I speak fluent Russian. My compulsory Soviet military service did a lot to improve that. I think *any* new language you can learn is a good thing, and I certainly use it a lot in my current work, which is in a Russian quarter of the city."

Both Tula and Pekka spoke excellent German and preferred using it over Russian or English.

Economic change was progressing quickly in Tallinn. Less than a decade after independence it was hard to find any signs of Soviet occupation, and loan interest rates were close to those in Western Europe.

---

25. Other sources estimate that over 20,000 were deported. There are about 1 million ethnic Estonians living in the country today.

"The government authorities are very eager to join NATO and the European Union. Perhaps too eager — they seem to be spending a lot of money to revamp the military in order to comply with NATO standards. But, then, it's always possible that there could be a change in administration in Russia which might pose a threat to Estonian independence."

"Most people are supportive of joining the European Union. Only about 30% of the people prefer a more isolationist approach, but this seems to be the less educated segment of society, which doesn't necessarily understand economics as well. We're too small to have an efficient economy on our own. Still, with respect to farm products, many people would like to maintain Estonian national production. Perhaps this has something to do with national security and self-sufficiency. But there is also a fear of chemicals in the foodstuffs. For example, much has been made recently of the use of such substances by Dutch farmers."

Old Traditions Reborn

Maiasmokk Café on Pikk Street in Old Town Tallinn was established in 1864. The wood-paneled walls were carved with Ionic columns and inlaid with mirrors. Patrons chose their pastries and coffee or tea at the efficient, busy counter, then found a place to sit anywhere they could, which often meant sharing a table with strangers. Across the table from me, a professorial-looking old man with coke bottle glasses was reading a newly-minted hardback in Estonian on the Nazi SS.

The tourists seemed to have discovered the place, but had not overshadowed its indigenous Nineteenth Century atmosphere.

CHAPTER 7

TO FINLAND

Tallinn, Estonia, July 23.

The Tallink hydrofoil ferry to Helsinki looked like an airplane inside: two dozen rows of cushy blue seats, carpeted aisles, hostesses in short skirts and duty-free shopping for the international crossing. Businessmen were reading newspapers and working on their laptops; children were pressing their noses against the window. There were life vests under the seats and emergency exit diagrams in the seatback pockets. The engines revved up at precisely 7:30 a.m. and the hostesses came around to take drink orders.

As soon as the ship left the protection of the harbor for the open waters of the Gulf of Finland, it hit large sea swells. Those who braved a walk down the aisle (no seatbelt signs here) lunged to and fro to keep their balance. A small boy in the next row began to wretch loudly. I gripped the seat arms and prayed for the one-and-a-half hour voyage to pass quickly.

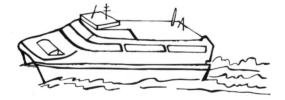

PART III

THE FAR NORTH

FINLAND

CHAPTER 1

NORTH TO THE ARCTIC CIRCLE

Helsinki, Finland, July 25.

The train platform in Helsinki Station was newly asphalted. Unlike the ridiculously low centrally-planned ticket prices of the Ukrainian and Belarussian railway systems, the overnight ticket to Rovaniemi made a noticeable dent in my wallet. Also unlike the tickets on the former Soviet railways, I could acquire it with a credit card.

Everything about the interior of the train was a night-and-day difference from the Soviet-built cars. The bunk beds in the sleeping car were stacked three high in single-sex compartments. The car was more than half empty, and I had no compartment mates. A sink in the corner of the compartment could be closed to form a table. The medicine cabinet above the sink was stocked with small

---

Expensive Finland

Finland was a land of sticker shock after the travel bargains in the Baltics. Prices were triple those in Estonia, the most expensive of the Baltic countries. Ice cream bars were close to $3 and ordinary restaurant lunches topped $20. In the capital city of Helsinki, English was the common language between natives and visitors from throughout Western Europe.

---

cartons of spring water and packages of liquid soap. The small trashcan was lined in plastic. A thermostat allowed the compartment residents to choose their own comfort level, which could then be verified by the thermometer on the opposite wall. The compartment was equipped with 110 and 220 current. Thick towels hung neatly by the sink, and the beds were already made up with fresh sheets. There was a card-key system to lock the compartment door. The WC was amply stocked with paper products, plus liquid soap.

Rovaniemi, Finland, July 27.

The train tracks ended at Rovaniemi, on the Arctic Circle. I transferred to the postal bus for the trip through the wild country farther north. After everyone on the bus was settled into the soft, new upholstery, the driver made his way down the aisle with a metal box on a shoulder strap, a combination change holder and charge card device, printing electronic receipts as he went along. Bus travel to the sparsely populated towns cost a small fortune, and passengers paid by the kilometer.

In addition to dropping bundles of mail at small settlements, the bus delivered backpackers to the backwoods and bread to the general stores along the route. The trees became smaller and smaller as the bus streamed northward along the two-lane road. The tundra began on the other side of Inari.

Chapter 2

Lapland:
Land of the Midnight Sun

Inari, Finland, July 27.

The postal bus dropped me off several kilometers south of town on the shore of Lake Inari. I rented a tiny log cabin. It was tight and strong, with a circuit breaker box, a smoke detector, double-paned glass windows and bug screens. There was a varnished knotty pine table and handmade rag rugs on the floor. A clothesline hung along the center apex, a second clothesline was over the porch and a third was strung between two trees next to the cabin. Apparently Finns do a lot of clothes washing, even on vacation. There was a cooking shelf with one pot, one pan, one teakettle, two dishpans, soap, a dishwashing cloth, a pot holder, a pot scrubber, a bucket with a dipper for drinking water and a bucket for trash. The bathhouse had rugs at just the right spots too, plus a squeegee for the floor. Even the sauna had a stack of wood ready on the porch in a small hand carrier.

RUSSIA

CHAPTER 3

THE BACK ROAD INTO RUSSIA

Raja-Jooseppi, the Finnish-Russian Border, July 29.

We seemed to be the only travelers at the Raja-Jooseppi border crossing, 250 kilometers north of the Arctic Circle. The guard on the Russian side dragged a set of heavy iron tire-puncturing spears out of the roadway to let the rattletrap 17-seat bus with its three passengers pull up to the passport control office. The four of us had completed one-sixth of our 300-kilometer journey from Ivalo, Finland to Murmansk, Russia, about half of which would be over washboard dirt and gravel roads.

We stepped out into the damp northern woods.

"Do we need to bring our suitcases?"

"No, they never ask for them," answered the driver. He found me a blank customs form and I filled it out. The customs agent pulled out a small metal seal chained to his belt, unscrewed the lid, dipped it in an ink pad and placed seals all along the currency disclosure section. I carefully folded the document and put it with my most precious papers.

Five minutes down the road from the passport control office was another roadblock, where a soldier boarded the bus and again inspected our passports. Perpendicular to the road was a tall, thick barbed wire fence with a "T" shaped section of barbed wire across the top. Along the fence line, a five-meter-wide strip of raked sand ran into the woods in both directions. It was just like the description given by a Cold War escapee in a Reader's Digest account I'd read as a child.

An hour later there was yet another checkpoint.

The driver pulled the bus over for a rest stop at a scenic lake in the woods, where the facilities consisted of a picnic table overlooking the water and a pair of wooden outhouses. The bus made a second, unscheduled stop to allow three wild falcons to finish their conversation in the middle of the road. A third stop quickly followed, due to a loud noise coming from the front wheel. The driver got out and banged around, and the noise disappeared. Then there was a fourth stop in the middle of nowhere for the driver to rummage behind the back seat for some unknown reason.

We whizzed right by two sets of hunters and fishermen with their thumbs out, but stopped to pick up another man dressed in camouflage and carrying a red metal backpack with canvas straps. He paid no money but shook hands with the driver.[26]

Winding down the hill through the industrial area north of Murmansk, the driver pulled over to let his friend in camouflage out and to deliver two coils of copper pipe to a man waiting beside the road.

---

26. It is customary for men who know each other to shake hands as a greeting and as a farewell. Male co-workers will exchange handshakes twice daily – in the morning when they arrive and in the evening when they leave. Women have no such custom, and it is relatively uncommon, though not inappropriate, for a woman to shake hands with a man. It is up to the woman to offer her hand. In some circles, when offered a woman's hand, a man will kiss it rather than shaking it. Men who are more self-assured or of higher rank tend to do this more often.

CHAPTER 4

MILITARY MURMANSK

Murmansk, Russia, July 30.

Murmansk was rusting heavily. Green grass and purple wildflowers had invaded the home port of Russia's Northern Fleet. Private enterprise was sparse, and ugly Soviet-built edifices still housed state stores offering the cheap, shoddy goods that no one would buy if they had a choice.

Labor was obviously cheap as well. On the main boulevard, two young men were spackling a five-story building. They had no scaffold. Rather, each was suspended from the eaves by a long rope with a bucket tied to the end, swinging like a pendulum. The end of each swing brought them within arm's length of the building, allowing them to reach out with their trowels and take a swipe at the exterior wall. The force of their contact with the building would send them away in another long arc.

I took the #1 bus (the "only one," the locals called it) out nearly to the end of the line and looked around for the Maritime Museum. It was supposed to be next to the Naval Officer's Club. Because it was a military area, I tried to look like I knew where I was going, but before long a distinguished-looking gray-haired man in a dark uniform with a lot of stripes on the sleeve placed himself on a course to intercept me.

Uh oh, should I reach for my passport?

Nope, he only wanted directions.

After asking for directions several times myself and stepping over paint cans and scaffolding, I came to the museum entrance. No one was around. I climbed the echoing staircase and called out.

"Hellooo!"

A woman on the third floor burst into chatter. "Come right in, come in. A ticket is five roubles." I handed her the money. Using a ruler as a guide, she tore off a page-long strip of five receipts printed on brown tissue paper, each one reading 'Ministry of Defense – USSR – concert ticket – one rouble.' I seemed to be the only visitor in the museum.

"Oh, you *must* take a guided tour," said the ticket seller. "The woman who gives them is very good. The price for foreigners is 60 roubles."

"It's not right to charge foreigners more than citizens for the same service."

"Maybe she can do it for less because the boss isn't here today." She dashed downstairs and reappeared a few minutes later. "How about 25 roubles?"

"Oh, all right."

She tore off five more pages of tissue paper receipts and handed them to me. Moments later, a young woman with a wooden pointer appeared, and for the rest of the afternoon held forth on the heroism and tragedy embodied in the canvas and metal chunks of maritime memorabilia before me. Amid a long history of submarine disasters in the icy Barents Sea, I heard the story of the long and courageous siege in blocking the Fascists at the northern tip of Norway during the Great Patriotic War.

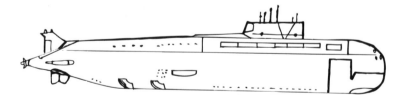

CHAPTER 5

KIZHI ISLAND

Petrazavodsk, Republic of Karelia, Russia, August 2.

There were no checkpoints or border guards as the overnight train from Murmansk passed southward through forests and lakes and entered the Republic of Karelia, a semi-autonomous region of Russia between Murmansk and Saint Petersburg. Karelians, relatives of the Finns and Estonians, were edged out eight to one by ethnic Russians in the republic, but still managed to give an ethnic flavor to the capital city of Petrozavodsk, where administrative buildings bore signs in both Karelian and Russian.

Petrozavodsk lay on the shore of Lake Onega, scene of a great battle during World War II. But Kizhi Island, in the middle of this enormous waterway, showed no scars of war. It was a slice of rural paradise, an open-air museum of wooden churches and peasant homes among hayfields, far from city sounds, surrounded by blue waters and rimmed with green reeds.

Getting to Kizhi Island and back was a trick. During the high summer season, hydrofoil passenger ferries made the long trip several times a day, but tickets had sold out long before I arrived in town. I wandered down to the end of the dock, found a boat due to leave in an hour and hung out conspicuously while hoards of lucky ticket-holders boarded.

Five minutes before departure time a megaphone crackled from the bridge. "OK, we'll take fourteen people without tickets." There was much pushing and shoving, but I was at the front of the line and, by the time a crew member's burly arm went down across the gangplank, I was on the boat. I bought a ticket at the on-board booth.

It was well worth the effort. The intricately carved wooden onion domes of Kizhi's Orthodox churches were some of the most picturesque in all of Russia.

The sun was low in the summer sky when the last ferry of the day pulled into the dock at Kizhi Island for the return trip to Petrozavodsk. By then, the crowd of ticket-less merrymakers had swelled substantially, as those who had arrived on several morning boats had lingered to enjoy a wonderful summer day to the fullest.

I took up a position on the end of the dock early and clung to the railing while those with pre-booked tickets fought their way through the stand-by throng. Then a sea of bodies surged relentlessly, and I nearly took an unscheduled dip in the lake despite the "no swimming" signs. Carried through by the crowd, I somehow ended up on the right side of the railing, and watched with relief as the boat shoved off, leaving a number of holiday-makers to spend an impromptu night camping on the island.

CHAPTER 6

MILKING TOURISTS IN
SAINT PETERSBURG

Nevskii Prospect, Saint Petersburg, Russia, August 4.

Brown smoke hung over the city so thickly that it blotted out the sun.

"It's the peat bogs burning," said a local lawyer whom I met for lunch. "When it gets this hot, they spontaneously combust. It doesn't happen often — It hasn't been this hot in fifteen years."

The air was fresher inside the House of Books on Nevskii Prospect, where I found a copy of the 1993 Russian Constitution. What a find! It contained a provision granting foreigners and stateless persons the same rights and obligations as Russian citizens, unless otherwise provided by federal law.[27] Museums and other tourist establishments were charging foreigners two to ten times the rates paid by Russian citizens, though exceptions were often posted for citizens of the Commonwealth of Independent States and the 'near abroad,' i.e., former Soviet citizens. I decided to do a test case or two.

The first stop to test the rule of law was the ticket booth of the Church of the Savior of the Blood, an 'Architectural Monument'[28] resembling a large version of Saint Basil's Cathedral.

"One ticket please." I shoved the 'citizen's' price through the window.

"Where do you live?"

"In Kiev." (Time to practice Deposition 101 training. Answer the question that's asked – don't volunteer information.)

---

27. Article 62, paragraph 3.

28. During the Stalin era many Russian churches were renamed 'Architectural Monuments' and religious services were suspended.

"Oh, ok, here you go," said the clerk. "You sure fooled me. It's amazing: the way you spoke, you sounded just like a foreigner."

Someone should clue her in that Ukrainians are now foreigners as well. I decided not to be the one to pour salt in any wounds — it's tough being a has-been empire.

The second test of the rule of law came at the hydrofoil port on the Neva River offering service to Peter the Great's ostentatious palace, *Petrodvorets*. It proved to be a more formidable opponent, though the foreigners' price was merely double the price for Russian citizens.

I slid 80 roubles through the hole in the window.

The cashier pushed them back. "I need 160."

"Why?"

"Because you're a foreigner."

I hadn't said a word. Did I have 'Foreigner' stamped on my forehead?

I pulled out the Constitution and opened it to Article 62.

"Look," I pointed. "Foreigners have the same rights as Russian citizens."

"Don't bother me with that. I don't make the rules here, you'll have to talk to the boss."

"Where *is* the boss?"

"Over there." She pointed to the hydrofoil.

I walked over. Three young men with life jackets and work gloves were standing around the gangplank.

"Where is the boss please?"

"Here," hollered a double-chinned man in a white shirt, poking his head out the cockpit window. "What do you want *me* for."

"I'm trying to buy a ticket for 80 roubles."

"I don't *sell* tickets. You have to buy them from the lady over there."

"She won't sell me one for 80 roubles."

"Of *course* not – you're a *foreigner*."

"The Constitution says you can't discriminate against foreigners. Here, have a look." I held up the book.

64

He swatted a fleshy palm in my direction. "To *hell* with the Constitution."

"You have to follow it."

"No we don't. We're a joint stock corporation."

"*Psst* – go over there and buy a ticket," interrupted one of the three young men in work gloves.

Had I somehow missed something? Had they seen a high sign in the boss's body language granting my request? I went back to the ticket booth, cut the line [29] and slapped down 80 roubles. "One ticket please."

"Who said?"

"The boys sent me back over here."

"I can't do it without authorization."

I looked back at the cockpit helplessly. The boss was certainly not giving helpful high-signs in our direction.

"Look, either you sell me a ticket for 80 roubles or I'll have to sue you for restitution of damages."

Grudgingly, a ticket appeared through the hole. I snatched it and strode back. Before I could reach the boat, the boss gunned the motor and roared off.

By the time I got to *Petrodvorets* on the next boat it was raining. The ticket booth at the garden entrance gate had a by-now-all-too-familiar message:

Citizens: 15 roubles.

Foreigners: 100 roubles.

I slipped 15 roubles through the window and a ticket came back. Boy, that was too easy. I got in line at the entrance gate and handed the ticket over to be torn.

"Excuse me, are you a foreigner?" a well-dressed woman taking tickets asked pleasantly. I really was going to need to look in the mirror to see if there was an 'F' imprinted on my forehead – I wasn't

---

29. This was in accordance with the prevailing Russian etiquette — I had already waited in the line once.

wearing Reeboks, a belt pouch or a day pack. But at least the issue could be neatly framed now.

"Why yes, I'm a foreigner but I have the same rights as..."

She held up an authoritative hand, cutting me off in mid-sentence, nodded knowingly and tore my ticket.

Hmm, was there a category of potentially loud-mouthed foreigners who had been placated with special privileges? Ukrainians, invalids, Great Patriotic War veterans; the list of persons entitled to reduced-price tickets seemed endless. It was obviously more expedient to carve out a new exception for one more group that might throw its weight around than to risk having to re-vamp the system for everyone. The palace was awash in tourists, many of whom were foreign. Following the existing law would seriously dampen the revenue stream, and lobbying the legislature to approve a legitimate two-tier pricing structure was not the Russian way.

CHAPTER 7

THE FED-UP RAILROAD MAN

Vitebsk Station, Saint Petersburg, Russia, August 7.

I stood on the suburban train platform at the 1904 Art Noveau Vitebsk railway station, surveying the schedule. A man spoke up beside me.

"Are you going to Pavlovsky Palace?"

"Yes, which train is it?"

"That one." He pointed. The schedule said it left in seven minutes.

"Where do you buy tickets?"

"Oh, that's a long way back through the station. You won't make it. Come with me, I'll explain — I work for the railroad." He pulled out a photo ID.

I followed him down the platform and onto the train without a ticket. We sat down on a wooden bench seat and the train pulled away.

"I'm going to my relatives' *dacha*.[30] It's further down the same train line. I'll show you to the gate and then catch the next train down there. Say, you don't know anyone in France, do you?"

"No."

"I want to go there to work. To do *anything*. Life here is very difficult. No one follows the law. Recently I crossed through Belarus in a car. We had to wait three days at the border; then they demanded five hundred dollars just for the right to *cross through* the country. We have a customs union with Belarus, so it's not supposed to cost anything. But what could we do?"

"Why do you want to go to France particularly? Why not, say, Germany, or…"

---

30. See sidebar *Dachas,* page 69.

"There's a different mentality in Germany. The French are very easygoing.[31] I need to save up money to bring back home here for my family."

"Look, everyone I've talked to wants to go to the West. It's impossible. There are 200 million people here.[32] You need to work on fixing the system *here*. It's up to the people here to demand that the law be followed." I explained my exercises with the Russian Constitution.

"If you do that, the next day when you come back they won't even speak with you."

"If everyone demanded it, they wouldn't have a choice but to follow the law," I said.

"You know, the laws themselves aren't that great here. There are certain people to whom the laws apply – that's us. Then there are people to whom the laws do not apply. They are the same people who make the laws, so they really don't care whether the laws make sense or not. We have some pretty crazy mixed up laws."

The train came to a halt at a station with an open-air market.

"There's a violation of the law right there." He pointed to a truck parked in the sun. A corner of the tarpaulin cover was thrown back, revealing crates of sausages. "Over twenty degrees[33] outside and they're selling un-refrigerated sausages. Maybe the seller *does* care about whether the people who eventually eat the sausages get sick, but he cares more about feeding his own family. Everyone is trying to make a living."

He walked me to the gate of the palace grounds and said goodbye.

---

31. This was probably code for being able to work illegally in France. Ethnic Russians love to lampoon the German lifestyle as being, in their view, overly serious, law-abiding and attentive to work and duty at the expense of fun and personal relationships. At the same time, many Russians (especially those who are getting the short end of the stick in the current free-for-all) wistfully long for the order and stability that the German system represents in their minds.

32. The population of Russia is about 146 million. Another 50 million live in Ukraine, and about 10 million more in Belarus.

33. Twenty degrees Celsius is about 68° Fahrenheit.

Dachas

The word dacha encompasses everything from a shack to a fabulous country home. The dachas of the wealthy New Russians and the government elite are often strictly recreational, while persons of more modest means grow a substantial amount of food on the small plots of land surrounding their dachas. Poor senior citizens may share an apartment with their children and grandchildren during the winter, but move to the dacha during the warm summer months to care for the garden. The younger generations spend weekends and vacations at the dacha.

CHAPTER 8

"THE CONSTITUTION DOES NOT APPLY TO US"

It was a good long walk from the entrance gate to Pavlovsky Palace. When I reached the palace the sign at the ticket booth read:

Citizens: 15 roubles

Excursions: 30 roubles

Foreigners: 140 roubles

I laid down 30 roubles. "Excursion, please."

"What was that again?"

She had heard me damn well; she just wanted another run at my accent.

"Excursion."

"I need 140 roubles."

I pulled out the Constitution.

"Don't even show that to me. Go talk to the Dispatcher."

I went to the next building and waded through a crowd of people putting on *tapochki*.[34]

"Where is the Dispatcher, please?"

The Dispatcher was engaged in a debate with an Asian tour group representative over the 140-rouble price, pointing out clauses in some kind of invitation letter. A compromise was finally reached at 70 roubles per person.

---

34. Museums in the former Soviet Union frequently do not have runner rugs on their lovely parquet floors. To save the floors from the damage of thousands of tourist feet, visitors wear the carpeting on their shoes, in the form of over-the-shoe slippers. In backwater museums the *tapochki* are frequently hand-stitched from thick quilted cotton cloth and tied with a string around the ankle. Those in some Saint Petersburg museums are literally cut out of carpeting. Large, floppy and crudely made, *tapochki* promote slipping and tripping, and would never be used in countries where personal injury lawyers successfully ply their trade. Museum employees and tour guides are exempt from wearing this unfashionable footwear.

Next it was my turn. I laid the Constitution in front of her.

She knew about it, didn't want to hear it, and looked around for an escape. She spied a card I was holding in my hand. "What kind of student are you?"

"I'm not a student."

"Who are you?" She was nervous now, craning her neck to try to see the card. I wasn't going to show it to her.

"I'm a foreign citizen, and I'm demanding my rights under the Russian Constitution."

"We don't have to follow the Constitution."

"Do you have a law which gives you the right to charge foreigners 140 roubles?"

She had no answer.

"How many of you are there?"

"One."

"Come with me." She stomped angrily back to the ticket desk. "Sell this woman a ticket for 15 roubles."

CHAPTER 9

MOSCOW BUREAUCRATS AND A TOUGH-TALKING RETIRED MILITARY MAN

OVIR – the Office of Visa and Registration, Moscow, Russia, August 10.

It was my third visit to the OVIR office and my second wait in the long line. According to all the guidebooks and the US Embassy, all visas needed to be registered with the authorities within three days of arrival. The day before I had been told that if I brought a letter from my sponsor (who had applied for the visa for me while I was still in Ukraine) and a declaration, my visa could be registered within 24 hours. That morning I had carefully copied by hand the required text for the letter and declaration, which was posted in a glass case at the OVIR office.[35] I had taken the text to my sponsor, who had carefully typed it up on company letterhead, signed it and stamped it with the purple ink seal of the company, a British firm with a representative office in Moscow. Next, I had waited in line at the bank to pay the visa registration fee of 16 roubles, 70 kopecks, copying the long series of OVIR bank account numbers in duplicate by hand on a tiny two-part brownish form. The bank clerk had torn the flimsy paper in half with the aid of her ruler, then stamped one half with her ink seal and returned it to me as a receipt.

After a 45-minute wait in line back at OVIR, it was my turn to lay my documents on the visa officer's desk. She began by scrutinizing the purple seal from my sponsor, then examined my visa, looking for discrepancies.

"It says here on the seal that this British firm is a *representative*

---

35. As in many other Russian state agencies, there were no photocopied forms available as handouts for the public.

72

office. Your visa does not say anything about that. I cannot accept this unless the head of the bureau allows me to. He's in Room 10. Usually he only hears problem applications on Mondays, but you can try getting him to approve it."

It was Tuesday. She could have gone to the director herself, but obviously wasn't going to trouble herself. The omission on my visa, typed by some unknown Russian bureaucrat, was the equivalent of leaving off the "Inc." at the end of the company name.

Metropolitan Moscow

Moscow was as large and complex as New York City, with a monstrous subway system and alternating pockets of wealth and rot. The Okhotnii Ryad (Hunter's Row) shopping mall, sunk into the ground below a central square right under the nose of the Russian Duma (Parliament), was as chic and polished as anything on Fifth Avenue. On the wide boulevards outside the center, speeding cars swerved to avoid potholes but not pedestrians, and roll-topped metal boxes in front of apartment buildings served as garages for the family car, lest it be reduced to a skeleton by desperate night-time piranhas.

From my room on the fourteenth floor of a boxy high-rise, I followed the signs down the hall to the door marked "Fire Escape." The door opened easily onto a small concrete balcony covered with cigarette butts (Russians usually don't smoke in their apartments or offices). I looked down a breathtaking 140 feet to the ground below. There were no stairs and no ladder.

On the street below, landscaping was under way in front of a marble-clad building under construction, and a well-dressed woman of sixty was nonchalantly stuffing spoonfuls of newly-dumped topsoil into a large plastic bag. Several more stuffed bags were already in her satchel.

I went to the director's office, knocked on the door and gingerly opened it, emitting a gust of laughter from the merry company inside.

"*Ne priom!*" (We're not receiving!) he hollered.

I closed the door. What did *that* mean? Wait until this person leaves? Or get lost?

A strongly-built gray-haired Russian man was also waiting outside the director's office.

"Where are you from?"

"America."

"Pfft! America. What does Clinton think he's doing, bombing Yugoslavia? He killed a lot of people and used atomic weapons. *NTV*[36] supported Clinton during the war and Yeltsin was too weak to stop him. It should never have happened.

"Our troubles started with Gorbachev," he continued. "He couldn't make a proper decision. He went to some school for decision-making set up by Margaret Thatcher. Just give me one little excuse and I'll be over there beating the crap out of Yeltsin. And so will 99 per cent of the rest of the people. I'm quite capable of doing that. Twenty-eight years I spent in the army. I ruined my health for this country, and what do I have to show for it? A tiny little pension. We're becoming controlled by the United States. The U.S. is trying to ruin our industries so that it can make a profit. Selling us all these Western goods — buy low; sell high. No one produces anything here anymore."

"Whom do you support instead as a Presidential candidate?"

"None of them! Our leaders are all puppets of the West now. They're all lining their own pockets and sending the money to Swiss bank accounts. They'll ruin an entire factory to put a $100 bribe in their pocket. We need someone like Stalin again." He left.

A pudgy Russian man ambled up and stopped outside the director's office. He was a messenger for a foreign company doing business in Moscow. He'd been sent down to OVIR to try to register some of the company's workers. "Look, this man looks like Saddam

---

36. NTV was the Russian television station with the most progressive programming and reportage at the time.

Hussein," he snickered, holding out an Iranian passport.

Forty-five minutes passed. Finally, the door to the director's office opened to emit the merry-makers. I approached again.

"*Ne priom*! I only take applications at 3:00 on Mondays."

"I won't be in Moscow by next Monday."

"That's *your* problem."

The director was about to slam the door in my face when he spied the pudgy man waiting as well. "Oh, you telephoned. Come right in."[37]

---

37. Quite likely, an exception was made for the pudgy man in exchange for money passing under the table. The woman who found the discrepancy between the corporate seal on the letter I had brought her and the wording on my visa, and decided to elevate form over substance, was probably looking to earn a little extra money as well. See sidebar *Corruption and Bribery,* page 76. I chose not to serve as an enabler, left without registering my visa and prepared to explain the circumstances if I were ever challenged. I never was.

Corruption and Bribery

Russia has an army of grossly underpaid bureaucrats, some of whom are earning very well indeed from their official positions, and others who are simply doing whatever it takes to feed their families. These millions are a powerful force against reform. Dotting i's and crossing t's to remedy fabricated discrepancies wastes such prodigious amounts of time that ordinary citizens regularly succumb to the path of least resistance by offering a gratuity.

While there will always be an element of corruption in any society, it propagates itself more vigorously in Russia than in other countries because citizens are more willing to feed it than to expose it. This tendency has many roots, including a perception by common people that they are outmatched individually; historical traditions which do not revere and reward whistle-blowing; the lack of an independent, uncorrupt judiciary to turn to for effective redress; the youth of the free press; a lack of experience on the part of ordinary citizens in organizing groups around issues of common interest; memories of brutal repression of those who questioned authority in the past; the fact that many citizens are living on the edge of survival and cannot afford to risk their positions to uphold a principle; and a class schism in which the government of the people has never been 'by the people' or 'for the people' which has led to a widely-held view that it is not morally reprehensible to violate laws promulgated by the state, including the laws against bribery.

CHAPTER 10

THE NUCLEAR ENGINEER-
TURNED SECURITY GUARD

Moscow, Russia, August 11.

I rode the Moscow metro nearly to the end of the line to visit an old friend. Volodya met me on the platform with flowers and with kisses on both cheeks. I hadn't seen him for several years, and he had put on weight.

We took a *marshrutnoye* to the *Akademgorodok* area where his apartment was located near the edge of the woods. On the way there, he pointed out the atomic research center where he used to work as a nuclear engineer.

"The government money dried up, and so did the work. There is still a little bit going on through some private contracts. There's even an American professor sitting there. Any military secrets we might have had are certainly gone by now." He laughed as he said it, for I was a friend, but there was an undertone of despondence bordering on resentment. The shining future had been lost.

Volodya's life had been marred by difficulties in the past few years. After the engineering work ended, he had started work as a travel agent. But the wages he was owed by the travel agency never materialized, so two years earlier he had quit to set up his own travel business. The day after he resigned, his seven-year-old son was hit by a car while crossing the road in front of their apartment.

"We rushed him to the Children's Clinic. He was unconscious for three months. Soon after the accident, I began to investigate how it had happened. There were skid marks for fifteen meters. It was the eve of the May Day holiday and the neighbors said the driver was drunk."

"But it turned out that he was a member of the police department, so no blood or breath tests were taken and the car disappeared.

My investigation was running into a brick wall. I gathered together all of the information I could and was going to go to the prosecutor the next day, but then I developed appendicitis and spent ten days in the hospital myself. While I was lying there I did a lot of thinking. The doctors were not sure at that point whether my son would live or die. I decided that if he died it was God's will, and a lawsuit would not bring him back. If he lived, we would somehow manage, and we would have more important things to worry about than the aggravation of a legal action."

We took a cool, wet path through the woods.

"They were giving my son lots of psychotropic drugs. My wife and I started hiding the drugs in the cupboard in his hospital room and he started to improve. Four months after the accident we brought him home. It's taken a couple of years, but he has nearly completely recovered now."

We stopped to buy a watermelon grown along the Volga near Astrakhan.

Volodya pointed to a concrete high-rise. "There's the apartment building I helped build in the early 90's. There was a program at the time under which I was released from work two days a week to work on the construction site. At the end of a couple of years I was supposed to be given an apartment, but then the financial troubles started, the money ran out and construction stopped. So I didn't get that apartment."

Volodya's new career was as a security guard for a foreign property management company. It was a long fall from nuclear engineer. He seemed to be more bitter than on his visits to California in the mid-1990's, when he had spoken eagerly about the possibility of starting his own business.

He was also very angry about the US invasion of Yugoslavia. War meant injuries, and injuries meant pain. There had been too much pain lately.

Chapter 11

The Dacha

Moscow, Russia, August 12.

In the middle of the "Ring Line" [38] platform of Moscow's *Prospect Mira* Metro Station, Natasha and her five-year-old daughter Katya were waiting for me with their gym bags packed. [39]

I followed them up and down escalators and on and off metro trains to the suburban train platform at *Savyolovskaya* Station. The local train released its brakes with a hiss as we hurried on board and found seats together on the varnished wooden slat benches. With the usual unassuming chivalry, a young man on the train hoisted my heavy pack onto the overhead rack.

Natasha and Katya looked so happy to be together. Natasha had been back for just ten days after a year of study in Germany. While her mother was studying in Germany, Katya was cared for by her great grandmother. Now that Natasha was back, there were five people – Katya, her mother, grandmother, great-grandmother and aunt, in a three-room apartment. No wonder they were eager to spend a few days at the family *dacha*.

Several days earlier, as I treated Natasha to coffee and pastries at a shiny new European-style café in Moscow, she explained the dilemma that she, like many other talented young Russians, was facing.

---

38. The Moscow metro system has a myriad of lines intersecting roughly at the center of town. To avoid the gridlock of all passengers trying to change at these central points, a loop called the Ring Line has been built around the center of town, so that passengers can conveniently transfer back out to another suburban line.

39. Russians normally travel very light, packing their belongings into nylon sports bags purchased at the open-air bazaars found in cities and towns throughout the country.

Professional jobs in Russia were few. She could return to Germany where she would be able to earn some money, but she would have to go without Katya because the German government would not issue her daughter a visa. "They're afraid we would immigrate, of course."

Natasha had a chilling tale to tell.

"Many others are in a much more difficult situation than we. There are families with lots of children who will sometimes sell one of the children in order to feed the rest."

"For adoption?"

"Yes, and also for organ donation. Adults do it too,[40] but children are preferred because they are generally healthier. It's easier to get a child across an international border than an organ."

"What countries are they going to?"

"The United States and Germany are the main ones."

The suburban train stopped often along the route, filling up fast until there was standing room only in the aisles as we rode northward into the green countryside. Vendors of ice cream, ball-point pens and shower curtains picked their way around the standing passengers to hawk their wares, ignoring a sign stating that such activity was strictly forbidden. A handicapped accordion player shuffled through playing a sad song and collecting coins.

An hour later, the train stopped among green hills. Natasha's father, Sasha, an ebullient, rosy-cheeked man, met us at the train stop. He stashed our luggage in the back of his two-door *Lada Niva* 4x4 and we flew lightly over the bumps in the road. (He held onto the steering wheel part of the time.) Marring the countryside, along the road were a number of small impromptu trash dumps, with discarded refrigerators, rusting cans and glittering glass.

"How do you like your 4x4?"

"It's great. I've had it two years and no mechanical breakdowns."

"What did it cost?"

"Seven thousand dollars. If I were to buy it today it would be

---

40. Russian television had carried an interview of a man planning suicide in exchange for $40,000, which would go to his young family.

four thousand."[41] (The rouble had plummeted from six to the dollar to 25 to the dollar since the August 17, 1998 crash.)

Four kilometers later we reached the *dacha* on the edge of a hillside, surrounded by a lush green vegetable garden and gnarled apple trees laden with small, misshapen but wonderfully sweet fruit.

The *dacha* consisted of three rather new buildings: a square, two-story brick main house; a small wooden summer kitchen with a long porch furnished with a glider swing and dining table; and a *banya*. The *banya* was a whole cabin in itself, with a long porch glassed in by wood-framed windows; a *stolovaya* with a red checkered tablecloth for vodka drinking; a wood-paneled bathing room with a shower and plastic wash basins hanging from pegs on the wall; and a wood-fired sauna. Upstairs over the sauna was a bedroom lavished with bearskins — heads and claws intact.

The rustic porch of the summer kitchen was the center of activity. We ate our meals there and sliced and diced all manner of produce on the long varnished wooden table: apples for apple sauce, potatoes for boiling, turnips and carrots for salad. All came fresh out of the black earth just steps away from the summer kitchen. On a side table, a large jar of cucumbers was set in salt water to turn into pickles. There was a white enamel sink at the end of the porch, and whoever took up dishwashing duty was rewarded with a view of the hillside, trees and valley below.

Not everyone in the neighborhood had such a well-equipped kitchen. As the sun rose, elderly women in headscarves and cotton print dresses trudged up the hillside carrying buckets of water home from the trickling stream at the bottom.

---

41. See sidebar *American Money*, page 19.

PART IV

THE GOLDEN RING

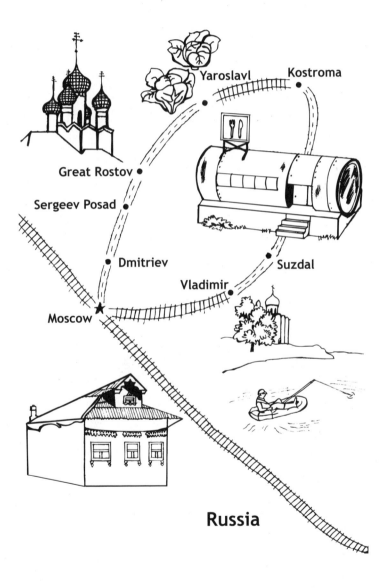

Yaroslavl

Kostroma

Great Rostov

Sergeev Posad

Dmitriev

Suzdal

Vladimir

Moscow

Russia

CHAPTER 1

TRAVEL LOGISTICS
CAN BE CHALLENGING

Dmitriev on the Moscow Canal,[42] Russia, August 14, 11:00 a.m.

A crowd of fifty was standing on the puddled parking lot when the forty-seat *Ikarus*[43] bus to Sergeev Posad pulled in and opened its front and back doors. Natasha elbowed her way up the steps and stood guard over a seat inside while Sasha, who had done a fine job of repairing my backpack with a socket wrench and some screws from his shop at the *dacha*, got the driver to open the luggage bin.

"It's her pack," Sasha pointed to me. "She's an American." It was a cue to the driver that I was to be looked after.

I climbed on board and squeezed past the people standing in the aisle to where Natasha was saving me a seat. After kisses on both cheeks she was off, waving with her mother and father as the bus pulled away.

The Golden Ring

The Golden Ring is a loop of cities northeast of Moscow that grew wealthy in previous centuries due to their advantageous location on the trade routes linking points throughout western Russia. Many early merchants contributed to the building of beautiful churches and monasteries in this area that still stand, making it a popular tourist route today.

---

42. Through a series of eight locks, the Moscow Canal links the Volga River with Moscow.

43. *Ikarus* buses, made in Hungary and painted a Soviet red and gold, are a ubiquitous means of public transportation throughout the former Soviet Union.

Sergeev Posad, Russia, August 14.

I arrived in Sergeev Posad at mid-day: plenty of time to see the monastery and then travel north in the evening to the next monastery at Great Rostov. The ticket agent said there would be a bus to Rostov at 7:30 p.m. I plunked down 40 roubles for a telephone card to make a reservation at "the" hotel in Great Rostov. Busy signal. [44] Eight more tries. Still busy.

I decided to visit the monastery and try to phone later. There was no left luggage room at the bus station. None at the train station next door, either. Maybe the monastery had one. I hopped on a city bus and asked the driver to let me out at the monastery.

When we reached the monastery entrance gate the driver shook his head apologetically.

"Sorry, I can't let you out here. This isn't an official stop and there is a traffic policeman right there."

He drove on for several blocks. Good grief, it would be a long walk back. My pack was getting heavy. How could there not be a bus stop in front of the main attraction in town?

Finally we came to a stop just across the street from the Hotel *Zagorsk*. Hey, maybe it had a luggage room.

I went inside. The woman at the front desk had hair of a hue that would cause alarm at the fire department.

"Do you have a luggage room?"

"Sorry, no," she said pleasantly.

"Is there one anywhere else in town?"

"Not that I know of, but you can leave it here behind the desk – I don't mind."

It was pilgrimage season at the monastery. The dark chapels were filled with a mesmerizing blend of harmonious, chanting singing and the scent of beeswax from hundreds of candles lit by the devout and placed in large brass holders near favorite icons. Long lines of dark-clad faithful filed past priests to pay their respects, and small,

---

44. Soviet era business telephones, most of which are still in place, usually do not "roll over" to a free line if someone is using the line you have dialed in on.

bent, elderly church women in cotton smocks and head scarves were in constant motion scraping mounds of soft warm beeswax and candle stubs from the brass holders into small buckets, to be re-melted into new candles.

The grounds of the monastery were filled with the impoverished devout, wearing their threadbare Sunday best and eating from small packets of food brought with them from distant farming villages. A few were already sleeping on benches; a room at the Hotel *Zagorsk* was not in the travel budget.

When I returned to the Hotel *Zagorsk* for my luggage I brought the desk clerk an orange[45] and interpreted for an agitated American tourist standing at the desk, concerned that the hot water did not work in his room. (He was not placated to learn that the hot water would be off for weeks all over town, and that there was nothing the front desk could do for him.)[46]

---

45. Traditional service people often do not expect tips and even turn them down, either because they are doing a favor out of kindness, or because it is better to accumulate good will on the chance that a return favor will be available to them in the future. This way of life worked quite well for many in the closed, static society of Soviet and pre-Revolutionary times. The mobile, monetized, pay-as-you-go modern world is seeping into the country, but the changes have not penetrated to all levels of society and may never do so. Small gift giving remains a well-established tradition. Thus, to show thanks for the desk clerk's kindness, an orange was a much safer, more personalized choice than a small tip.

46. See sidebar *Hot Water*, page 87.

Hot Water

In many parts of the former Soviet Union, hot water is provided centrally to the whole city or city-district, both as hot tap water and for steam heat. In summer, after the "heating season" ends, these systems are often taken out of service for repairs. This necessitates the summer closure of many swimming pools as well, which are heated off the same grid. As the infrastructure in the former Soviet Union continues to age and city housing authorities continue to be short of cash and spare parts, the periods without hot water may well grow longer. Some top-end hotels have installed their own hot water systems, or at least attached European-style instant electric water heaters to the showers in some of their rooms. Thus, if an administrator offers you a room with an "electric shower," it may not be as bad an idea as it sounds.

Some buildings, especially in outlying areas, are not hooked up to central hot water at all. Other buildings receive central hot water for the radiators but not for washing and bathing. Lucky (or well to do) apartment dwellers in such buildings have a kolonka, or individual hot water heater. The water heater may be fueled by natural gas (which is not available in all areas), electricity (as was Yuri's home-built milk can heater near Yalta), or wood (as in Velta and Evald's country cottage near Jekabpils, Latvia.)

In both the central and kolonka hot water systems, scale and flecks of iron in the pipes can be a problem. In central systems, the hot water flowing from the tap is often the same water that has coursed through the radiators. In my turn-of-the-century apartment in Kiev, which was fitted with a natural gas kolonka, scale would cause the hot water outflow pipe to clog and the water trapped in the kolonka to build in temperature to superheated steam. The pressure would then blow out the blockage in a burst of brown, spitting, hissing watery steam. I learned to step out from beneath the shower if it began to trickle while the tap was wide open.

Yuri, a consummate handyman, whose nine-year-old concrete apartment building in the Crimea suffered from rusting pipes as well, had solved the problem of iron flecks bursting out of his kitchen sink faucet and into his cooking water by wrapping a number of strong magnets around the spout of his kitchen sink.

Many municipalities, their tax bases in a shambles, are unable to keep up the maintenance on their systems, and pipes have been known to rupture and spew hot water inside building walls. Russian television reported a large sinkhole that formed around a hot water main which burst beneath a public street. A child fell in the hot pool and was badly scalded.

At seven o'clock that evening, back at the bus station, I went to the ticket counter.

"One ticket to Rostov, please."

"We don't know yet whether the 7:30 bus is going this evening. Go outside and wait at Platform 8."

I decided to burn up the telephone card, which would be useless once I left Sergeev Posad,[47] saying hello to the folks back home. No dice. The card was only good for making calls to points within the Commonwealth of Independent States.

I went outside. The station was crowded, and half a dozen people were waiting on a bench at Bus Platform 8. Seven forty-five arrived. Still no bus. The next scheduled one wasn't due for another two hours. I *could* go back to the Hotel *Zagorsk* and get a room with a cold shower.

A slender young man dressed in a black shirt and black pants and holding a bunch of keys came through the crowd.

"Anyone going to Pereslavl-Zalessky? I'm taking a *marshrutnoye* up there."

"How much?"

---

47. Russia and other parts of the former Soviet Union are plagued by a series of "baby Bells" whereby a microchip or magnetic strip telephone card will only work in the pay phones of the company which issued the card, which may be located only in one city. The inter-city and international rates charged by these telephone companies can be exorbitant.

"Thirty roubles [$1.20]. If you want to go, the van is parked over there."

Pereslavl-Zalessky actually seemed a good gamble. It was half way to Great Rostov. I could check out "the" hotel in Pereslavl-Zalessky and if, for some strange reason, it was packed with guests, I could go on to Great Rostov when (if?) the 9:30 p.m. bus came through.

I went over to the *marshrutnoye* van, where three people were already waiting. Forty minutes passed. The driver was still out scrounging for riders. I read all the signs plastered around the inside: 'Riders are obligated to pay a fare regardless of how much space they take up.' 'Fare: 2 roubles, 50 kopecks.' That was the in-city rate. The driver was moonlighting.

Finally the driver emerged from the crowd. I stepped out of the van.

"Are you planning to go to Pereslavl-Zalessky *tonight*?" I wondered if my sarcasm was coming through.

"Yes, I'm leaving right now."

The mini-bus sailed along the road for 60 kilometers to Pereslavl-Zalessky, passing lots of slow trucks. A slab of sheetrock flew off one of the trucks, smacked into our windshield and sailed away.

On the outskirts of town, the driver pulled to a stop at the side of the highway and turned off the motor.

"Aren't you going to the bus station?"

"This *is* the bus station."

Sure enough, it was.

"Do you want me to take you to the hotel?"

"Yes, please."

Chapter 2

The Best Hotel in Town

Pereslavl-Zalessky, August 14.

The *Pereslavl* Hotel did, of course, have rooms available. I surveyed the list of room types and prices posted at the desk.

"A room with a shower, please." I filled out a registration form and handed over my passport and visa.

The desk clerk pulled out a "foreigners" price list.

"I'm entitled to the same prices as a citizen." Paying an astronomical rate wasn't going to make the bed any softer or the water any hotter.

"Oh, because you live in Ukraine?"

"No, because of this." I pushed Article 62 of the Constitution through the window.

"Ah, I know about that." She pushed it back with hardly a glance. "But you're registered to live in Ukraine, are you not?"

"Yes, there is my visa and there is the registration stamp." I pointed in my passport.

She wasn't ready to acknowledge the Constitution, but gave me the citizen's price on account of the Ukrainian connection.

"Can you stamp my visa as well?"

"Certainly."

It was a long process. She had a box full of rubber stamps and a dried-up ink pad. She tried out a few stamps on scratch paper, licking them first to help coax a little more ink out of the pad. Finally she found the right one, rolled it neatly on my visa and handed it back to me.

I took the elevator to the fourth floor. No hot water in this hotel, either. The telephone was a black rotary-dial model hard-wired into the wall. So much for connecting to the Internet with the five-pronged converter plug I had finally found in a kiosk in a Moscow pedestrian underpass. The television was stuck on "loud" and the bathroom door handle was sitting on the table next to the television. A cockroach scampered across the clean white pillowcase. A dozen mosquitoes were hovering along the high ceiling. I stood on a chair and swatted at a few with a towel, releasing a cloud of plaster dust with each blow. Never mind. I slathered on repellant and went to bed.

Pereslavl-Zalessky, Russia, August 15.

At the front desk of the *Pereslavl* Hotel, the woman who had licked the rubber stamps into life had been supplanted by a heavyweight bleached blonde. She reluctantly took time out from her busy schedule of watching the men wandering in and out of the lobby cafe to call the bus station for me to learn the schedule, self-importantly admonishing the dispatcher that she was calling on behalf of a foreigner. Yes, there was a bus to Great Rostov in an hour and a half.

The bus station was a concrete building, painted pale green inside, with small honeycomb-like waiting areas. There were two ticket windows, each promising 24-hour service, save a brief 'dinner break' in the wee hours of the morning. I approached one of the windows.

"May I have a ticket to Rostov?"

"No, I can't sell them until the bus arrives."

The bus was due in 50 minutes. I took a seat in one of the concrete waiting pods. There were tired old men in French-style berets with their pants tucked into tall rubber boots, and women with kerchiefs on their heads guarding buckets of cucumbers. Several new people entered the station and asked loudly: "Who's last?"[48] I began to worry that I hadn't "gotten in line" properly, but it was too late to open my mouth now.

---

48. 'Who is the last one in line?' or 'Who is on the end?' This etiquette has been developed to deal with the frequent need to wait in slow-moving lines. Russians often place themselves in a line and then go off and do something else ☞

Forty-five minutes passed. I peeked outside. Sure enough, the bus to Rostov had arrived. I went back to the ticket window.

"*Now* may I buy a ticket to Rostov?"

"You don't buy the ticket here; you buy it from the bus driver. Hurry, the bus is about to leave."

Great Rostov, Russia, August 15.

The old wooden houses in Great Rostov, though sagging and leaning, had some of the most beautiful window frames and shutters in all of Russia, hand carved into something resembling wooden lace.

Inside the ancient monastery walls of Rostov was a small inn. When I appeared at the door, the matron on duty was hand-rolling short lengths of bathroom tissue from a new roll onto a pile of empty cardboard tubes.[49] I secured a room overlooking the stone perimeter wall and settled into the dark wood paneled television lounge to watch the *Duma* confirmation hearings. Members of the Russian Parliament were questioning the latest in a long series of Yeltsin nominees for prime minister – an urbane, highly articulate political unknown named Vladimir Vladimirovich Putin.

---

while the line moves along, "saving" their place by telling the person ahead of them that they will be back. They may leave the line simply to sit down, or, if there are two ticket counters, they may hedge their bets by getting in a second line that might move more quickly. It is also wise to ask this question when the structure of the line is less than clear.

49. Toilet paper is often in limited supply in Russia. Hotel bathrooms frequently have a small plastic box hung on the wall to hold torn strips of paper, and even when the usual kind of rolled paper is available, it is generally provided only in small quantities, on the theory that leaving more available to patrons will only encourage waste, or even theft. Public washrooms almost never stock paper in the stalls. In pay restrooms attended by a live person, the admission fee generally includes a small ration of paper handed out at the entrance. Because all manner of paper is used by the visiting public, each stall has a waste basket into which the visitor is expected to place used paper, rather than clogging the plumbing.

CHAPTER 3

THOSE NOISY CHURCH BELLS!

Yaroslavl, Russia, August 17.

At the Monastery of the Transfiguration of the Savior, a copy of an article from the *Northern Worker*, May 1, 1929, was posted in the bell tower:

> We, the workers of the Makhorochni factory, consider the decision of the City Council to prohibit the disorderly ringing of church bells on Easter to be fully supported, and protest the unjustified protest of the Public Prosecutor. No one can force thousands of working people to listen to this unnecessary noise on their day of rest. We ask that the prosecutor withdraw his protest. We want to relax in peace.
>
> The prohibition of the constant ringing of church bells is not unconstitutional. Catholic and Orthodox churches outside our borders, those in Leningrad and those who do not have bell towers, get along just fine without this noise....

Chapter 4

Through the Countryside to Kostroma

Yaroslavl Main Train Station, August 18, 3:18 p.m.

The local day train to Kostroma had two rows of varnished wooden seats, seating three persons each, varnished wooden window frames and no rest rooms.

The sky was clearing after several days of rain. Large cumulus clouds and the trunks of the birch trees along the train tracks were bright white in the late afternoon light and framed by brilliant green grass and leaves. We passed villages with onion-domed churches and small wooden houses. Each house had a wood-fenced yard. Some of the fences were planks; others simply straight tree branches or sapling trunks spaced close together. Gardens of cabbages, chard and cucumbers grew protected inside the fences, while chickens pecked outside on the grass.

The train made frequent stops in the countryside. A young woman in uniform selling tickets on board wore a "necklace" of perhaps 25 different small rolls of thin brown tickets, enabling her handily to tear off a ticket of the right price whenever she made a sale.

Kostroma, Russia, August 19, 7:00 p.m.

The *Volga* Hotel in Kostroma observed a strict two-tier room pricing system based upon the guest's nationality. Though the difference in price was less than ten dollars (other hotels were charging up to a hundred-dollar premium to foreigners), as usual I objected to paying the discriminatory premium to see how the issue would be handled. After enormous resistance, an exception was made for me in view of my Ukrainian connection. Two weeks into my experiment with the rule of law and not one person had yet acknowledged that the Constitution applied to them.

I crossed the lobby, got on the elevator, pushed in the "7" button until it clicked, then pushed the "go" button. The small metal cabin creaked slowly upward. "Manufactured in the Experienced-Experimental Elevator Factory – Moscow" read a plaque posted on the cabin wall.

The key desk on the seventh floor landing was empty. The only sound came from the churning motor of a padlocked refrigerator with a glass front door, exhibiting the products available for purchase from the *dezhurnaya*: various kinds of beer, soft drinks, juice, mineral water, salted nuts and sliced sausage.

"Hellloooo…" I called.

"Here I am."

I found a cheery floor lady in the room behind the fridge, poring over a ledger of hand-written numbers with a small hand calculator. She took my guest card and escorted me to a room with a view over the Volga River. A barge and tugboat were passing.

"I'll bring you a towel in a little while. The truck came today for the washing and it hasn't returned yet."

CHAPTER 5

A COMFORTABLE
RIDE TO SUZDAL

Kostroma, Russia, August 20, 11:15 a.m.

At the bus station, the ticket lines were ten persons deep each. That would mean waiting through at least twenty people, by the time all the line-jumpers with special situations cut in. I'd miss the 11:30 bus for sure.

I went out to the parking lot and waited for the bus to pull in. It turned out to be a mini-bus. A bus station matron appeared and began tearing computer-printed sales receipts, while a dozen people piled into the passenger area of the small van and covered every square inch of floor space with luggage. I approached the large motherly ticket-tearer.

"Can I buy a ticket here? The lines are long inside and I'm afraid I won't make it in time."

"Are you Polish, dear?"

"No, American."

"Certainly you can. Driver, open the front door. We'll put our *Amerikanochka*[50] right up here in front. Have a nice trip."

I reached for my wallet.

"Don't pull your money out *here*," said the driver.[51]

A young woman approached the driver and prevailed upon him to carry a letter to Vladimir for her.[52] Then the bus pulled out, stop-

---

50. A diminutive of *Amerikanka* (American woman). The diminutive is used to indicate endearment.

51. By taking my money "down the road" and not issuing a receipt, the driver would be able to pocket the $1.75 fare for the three hour trip.

52. See sidebar *Postal Service,* page 97.

ping on the edge of town for two more passengers. One shared the front seat with me and the other somehow, improbably, squeezed into the back.

Postal Service

In many former Soviet countries, people do not use the official postal system if they can find an alternative. For business-to-business correspondence within the same city, a driver or other low-level employee is often dispatched to deliver letters and parcels by hand. If the letter needs to go to another city, the sender may give it to someone who is travelling in that direction, and then telephone the recipient to let them know it is on its way and make plans for a rendezvous.

An indigenous form of overnight mail service between cities is to send a driver to the train station to seek out a provodnitsa on an overnight train to the destination city, entrust her with the package, and note the number of the train car in which she is travelling. The recipient is then notified, and sends a driver to meet the incoming train the following morning.

The sending of correspondence through the regular mail is so rare that many citizens are confused as to where the sender's and recipient's addresses are to be written on the envelope. (The Ukrainian postal service now requires envelopes to be addressed in the Western fashion, with the recipient's address in the lower right hand corner and the sender's address in the upper left.) One Russian told me that, because all mail is sorted by hand, it did not much matter whether the recipient's information began with the destination city or (as Westerners do) with the name of the recipient.

We passed green fields, birch groves and small wooden houses with fancy gingerbread-carved window frames. A diner appeared at the roadside. It was the size of a train car and the shape of a perfect cylinder — probably made from a grain silo turned on its side. A blue and white knife-and-fork highway sign had been "privatized" by the diner owner and mounted on the roof.

We stopped an hour later for the driver to add a couple liters of water to the radiator, and an hour and a half after that at the Ivanovo bus station.

The Ivanovo stop turned into an impromptu lunch break. Boiled eggs appeared from the back of the van, along with *butterbrod* (sandwiches made of slices of dark bread, fatty *kolbasa* and cheese) and small green homegrown apples, supplemented by bottled beer and waffle-cookie ice cream sandwiches from the bus station vendors.

Half an hour further down the road we reached the pastoral town of Suzdal.

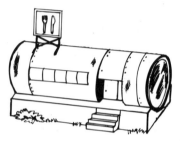

CHAPTER 6

IDYLLIC SUZDAL

Suzdal, Russia, August 19.

The passengers from the mini-bus said farewell as if we were old friends when they left me at the bus station on the edge of town. I approached a clutch of locals waiting for the bus into town, inquired about the schedule, and was instantly taken under their wing.

The Suzdal city bus pulled in moments later. No conductor on this route – instead, there was a large window into the driver's cab through which tickets were sold. [53]

"Yuri Ivanovich! [54] I want to come talk to you tomorrow night about *land reform*," an elderly man addressed the driver as he boarded the bus.

Wow, was I hearing bold grass-roots activism?

No, just a pensioner with a sense of humor. It turned out that Yuri the driver, who looked to be of retirement age himself, no longer had time to work one of his garden plots,[55] now that he was driving a bus. So his fellow senior citizen, who had more time on his hands, wanted to discuss a land use arrangement.

---

53. On most Soviet-era city busses, the driver's compartment is glassed in or walled off from the passenger area. Whatever the reason, it certainly improves safety by keeping jam-packed passengers from accidentally lurching into the driver's personal space.

54. Older people are referred to in conversation, and addressed, by their first name and patronymic. For men, the patronymic ("son of _____") is formed by adding -*vitch, -evich* or -*ovitch* to their father's first name. For women, the patronymic ("daughter of _____") is formed by adding -*vna, -evna* or -*ovna* to their father's first name.

55. See sidebar *Garden Plots,* page 100.

Garden Plots

Weekend gardens are a popular tradition among apartment dwellers throughout Central and Eastern Europe. During Communist times, Soviet factories and institutions provided garden plots as a fringe benefit to their employees, allowing them to stay in touch with their peasant roots and, importantly, to supplement their winter food supply with potatoes and other vegetables and fruit. Many former Soviet citizens retain the use of these parcels today. Some garden plots are merely patches of land the size of a two-car garage. (In Ukraine, the borders of these land plots are traditionally planted with sunflowers or corn as a sort of natural picket fence.) Dachas are built on larger garden plots.

The twentieth century had blissfully ignored Suzdal. Cows grazed peacefully in the tall grass beside the church walls and ducks paddled in the clear stream running through town. Nearby, a peasant scythed hay to cart home to his animals. Dozens of steeples, many crumbling, stood as monuments to the town's importance on a major trade route several centuries ago.

It was the eve of the 975th anniversary of Suzdal and there were lots of visitors. I finally found the last empty room in town, at a tumbledown monastery on Lenin Street. It seemed that the monks had abandoned the place for more comfortable quarters.

"Let me show you the room before you decide to take it," said the administrator. She led the way to the top floor and pointed to a large brown hole in the ceiling plaster. Water was slowly dripping into a paper cup sitting on the desk below.

Outside in the courtyard, late in the long summer twilight, a large group of workmen gathered around a decayed turret in the monastery wall. Several men were perched precariously on the turret itself: one at the top of the spire, painstakingly cementing terra cotta-colored replacement tiles in place; several more balanced along the top of the wall, where the tile roof of the spire began to rise to a point. These men served as the middle link of a "tile brigade," receiving tiles one-by-one from below and carefully handing them up to their mate above. Aside from a pair who were chipping old mortar off a pile of tiles in the courtyard, most of the men were lounging against an ancient truck or standing around observing the work above, seemingly not "on the job," but simply to enjoy being outdoors with their buddies on a summer evening.

CHAPTER 7

THE STALINIST LIBRARIAN

Vladimir, Russia, August 20.

It was a gray, rainy day as the bus from Suzdal made its way through the industrial part of town. Fat, hissing, rusty pipes wound along and over the streets, past huge cooling towers and red-and-white striped smokestacks. It was ugly. Had it not been for an acquaintance I wanted to look up in town, I probably would have gotten on the next train out of there. I looked at the schedule: the last direct train of the day to Moscow left in two hours. I'd give the city that long.

I entered the train station and descended the stairs to the dark, depressing basement, where there was a row of sturdy gray metal lockers with choose-your-own-combination knobs. The money slots in the lockers demanded 15 kopecks. That was a long time ago – before hyperinflation shrank the posted price to one-half of one cent. I stashed my bag in a locker and handed the attendant a ten-rouble note for a *zheton* to close it, then set out on foot to find a member of the university library staff who had visited me in California several years earlier. I could have bought a plastic telephone card for Vladimir at one of the kiosks, but I did not have a telephone number for her, and there were no phone books in the telephone booths along the street. I would either have to find the main telephone and telegraph office and hope for a helpful clerk, make my way to the university in person and ask around, or check into an Intourist hotel and let the staff help me. But I hadn't decided I wanted to stay yet.

The main street of Vladimir was a bit less depressing than the train station, and got better and better as I went along. A museum appeared; then a cathedral. OK, I'd give the place one night. I found a small café serving *blinchiki*. Passing up the pancakes topped with translucent orange caviar of uncertain vintage, I ordered three *blinchiki* drowned in honey and a cup of coffee with hot milk, which arrived pre-sugared to the sticky sweet Russian taste.

Three young women at the next table were also enjoying *blinchiki*, along with sliced tomatoes and cucumbers and a bottle of cognac. When I had finished my meal I approached them.

"Hello, *priyatnaya apetita*."[56]

"Thank you."

"Can you tell me how to get to the university?"

"We certainly can! Take the "eight-er" from across the street."

"Thank you." I turned to leave.

"Wait! We can even tell you how many stops it will be." The three of them counted on their fingers, rattling off the names of each of the stops between the café and the university. They seemed pleased to be helpful and proud of their knowledge of their home town.

"Get off at the twelfth stop."

"Thank you."

I caught the trolley bus, paid the conductor 1 rouble 50 kopecks for a thin grayish ticket, and, standing in the crowded aisle, muffled in by arms and coats and hats, quickly lost track of how many stops we had made and how many traffic lights we had hit. The conductor helped out.

"There are two 'University' stops. Which *korpus* do you need?"

"The one with the research library."

"Gosh, I don't know. That library wasn't built when I attended the university." She consulted a younger passenger, then pointed out the right building as the tram came to a halt.

I bought a small box of chocolates at a kiosk across the street before going into the building, then approached the "entrance lady."

"Raisa Mikhailovna?"

---

56. "I wish you a pleasant appetite." It is considered polite to say this any time you walk in on someone who happens to be eating, whether or not you intend to have further conversation with him or her. If you have been sitting with someone while having a meal, it is polite to say "thank you" when you rise to leave. This is short for: "Thank you for the company," indicating that you appreciate having had someone to converse with over the meal.

"First door to your left."

Behind the first door to the left was a high-ceilinged office with a heavily scuffed parquet floor. Raisa and a colleague sat at small wooden desks, facing each other across the small room. Each had a rotary telephone joined to a single telephone line with a loud musical bell. Neither had a computer on her desk. An electric teapot was balanced on a heavy wooden chair nearby, with the cord plugged into a round socket midway up the wall.

It was 2:30 p.m., half an hour before closing time on Friday. Raisa had the day off, but had dropped by to re-pot one of the office plants. She immediately set about telephoning to find out if one of the university's guest apartments [57] was available. The hot water was off in one, and no one knew whether the other one was free, or whether another visitor would be arriving from Moscow.

Three o'clock arrived. Closing time. Raisa summoned one of her employees, Yevgenia, into her office.

"Can you please take care of our guest from San Francisco this afternoon?"

"Certainly, but what do you need me to do?"

"Take her home with you, let her have a bath and feed her. I will telephone at 6:30 p.m. I need to find out whether the apartment is available, and then find my husband with the car so that he can fetch her bag from the train station."

"All right, but I'm leaving for the *dacha* tonight. She could stay in my apartment. Also, you need to give me some money to buy food."

I protested that I could certainly buy all the food necessary, but it was to no avail. Raisa marched over to a wall safe, pulled out a 100-rouble note and handed it to Yevgenia.

"You're our guest here."

Yevgenia lived with her cocker spaniel, walking distance from the library, in a well-decorated apartment on the eighth floor. She had a living room, bedroom, kitchen, bath and hallway. Everything was clean, newly wallpapered and neatly organized. She struck a

---

57. It is common for large institutions to have their own apartments or even their own hotels for employees and others visiting from out of town.

match and lit the two-burner gas stove to heat water for tea.

"Green tea or black?"

She dumped a freshly purchased kilo of sugar into a canister and apologized that she was out of toilet paper. ("I keep forgetting to buy it.") She washed two tomatoes and a homemade dill pickle under the tap, and put them in a bowl on the table.

"Do you like *kasha*?"

"Yes."

She pulled a pot of boiled buckwheat groats out of the tiny refrigerator, poured a generous amount of sunflower oil into a heavy iron frying pan, and poured a heap of groats on top. "Wait, I'll cook some more," she spooned in some extra. "The dog is hungry too." On a salary of about twenty dollars a month, purchasing imported pet food at the bazaar was not in Yevgenia's budget.

After sautéing the groats in oil, she dumped half of them into the dog's dish, chopped up a tomato, stirred it in, added a large amount of salt and placed the dish on the floor. The spaniel gobbled up the groats and looked at me attentively while I was eating mine.

Shortly after 7:00 p.m., Raisa called to say that she and her husband would be by shortly. We went downstairs to meet them.

"The elevator button doesn't work from this floor," explained Yevgenia. "We'll have to walk down a flight. It's our government's fault. They are supposed to come and fix these things for us."

Yevgenia and Raisa gave me the grand tour of town, showing me all the expensive new bank buildings that had been built in the last few years. "And none of them has any money to lend."

Raisa's husband, Alexei, a solidly-build, handsome 40-year-old in the military service, did all the driving. He owned a dark blue one-year-old *Volga* sedan and drove with an opinion — lurching forward, accelerating and slamming on the brakes. "There's water in the gas," he explained.

While Raisa and Yevgenia were showing me the sights, Alexei sat in the car, listening to tapes on the excellent sound system and ensuring that the vehicle came to no harm from hooligans while parked on the city streets.

"I'm an optimist," he said. "We need to do a few things to fix the economic system, but I think in a few years things will get much better."

He drove us back to Yevgenia's apartment, where Alexei and Raisa said good night. Yevgenia's trip to the *dacha* had fallen through, so she would sleep on the bed in the kitchen as usual, while I took the bedroom, which was usually rented to a student (now away for the summer holidays.) We had a supper of *pelmeni,* sliced tomatoes, dill pickles and fresh sliced garlic. Next came green tea, *pechenye,* applesauce and cheese. We sat for several hours at the kitchen table, talking about life in Russia today.

"I have nothing bad to say about the system we used to have [under Communism]. I never felt myself "un-free." Rather, I felt safe; protected. I studied at night school and never thought twice about walking out alone at night. We used to go strolling. Now I would never walk anywhere at night. I used to be able to afford to go on vacation; to go to a restaurant twice a month. Now I can buy food and clothing, but not much more. Everything you see around here — the refrigerator, the dishes — all of this is left over from the old days."

"This apartment was issued to me," she continued. "I don't have to pay rent, but I do have to pay a monthly fee for hot water, garbage, gas, light and so forth. The prices of these keep going up even though my salary does not. But it's much worse for young families. Nowadays the government isn't building apartments any more; the only way a young family can obtain one is to buy it. And with what money? No one provides credit for such things, and especially not long-term credit of 20 to 25 years. So young families continue to live with their parents. They will not have anything until they have worked their whole lives, and then their lives will be spent."

Yevgenia had a legal right to privatize her apartment, but, unlike Irena, the woman I had stayed with in Lithuania, had chosen not to.

"It's lots easier if you're simply *propiskaed*.[58] Then when you die,

---

58. A *propiska* was a document issued by the Soviet authorities to indicate that a person had a right to live in a particular apartment and had legal residence

your apartment just goes to your son, or your grandchild. If it's been privatized, you have to go through a lot of paperwork and your grandchild can't own it unless you pay a huge tax."

How could a nice middle-class woman like Yevgenia be supportive of Stalinism?

"I was born in 1939," she explained. "I grew up during a period when, just after the Great Patriotic War, things kept getting better and better. Coming from that perspective, it's hard for me *not* to be supportive. I was never a Communist, but I was a patriot. I guess I still am."

"Did you ever experience people close to you being oppressed by Stalin?"

"No, I never personally knew anyone who suffered under Stalin, though I know that he even got rid of those in his inner circle. You know, he himself only had one shirt and one pair of boots. He never let his daughter dress up in fancy clothing. Nowadays the people you see driving around the city, stuffing their Swiss bank accounts – it's impossible to recognize them as our own people."

"In Latvia and Lithuania I was told that one-third of the population was lost or sent to Siberia during Stalin's rule."

"Remember that that was war and Russia was victorious over Latvia and Lithuania. They had sided with the Germans. It was Russia's right as the victor to punish them."

"What do you think of the war in Chechnya?"

"It's a repeat of Afghanistan. Our people are not protesting against the government's waging of the war. It will go on for 30 years. It will be smothered, then flare up again and again."

We talked about the difficulties of foreigners investing in the former Soviet Union.

"I lived in Tashkent [59] for 25 years. The Germans started going

---

in the city. One generally could not obtain a *propiska* without a job in the city, nor a job without a *propiska*. This made it very difficult for people to move during Soviet times.

59. Tashkent is the capital of Uzbekistan, a former Soviet republic in Central Asia and now an independent country.

in there to invest in the early 90's, but recently they have stopped. I can imagine why. The Germans are very exacting and their expectations of their counterparts are high. But the Uzbekis have a cultural trait that does not permit them to say 'no I cannot do that for you.' It's always 'hup, hup, yes, of course,' and then you wait and wait and wait and nothing happens. It probably drove the Germans crazy."

CHAPTER 8

RELIGIOUS REVIVAL

The next day, Yevgenia and I took the trolley bus to Raisa's and Alexei's apartment for lunch. Raisa, Alexei and their two sons had a two-room apartment plus kitchen and bath. One room was the living room / parent's bedroom and the other room was the dining room / boys' bedroom. All the beds folded up into sofas and armchairs during the day. The hallway and balcony of the small apartment were filled with boards and other construction materials that the family was stockpiling in preparation for an upcoming do-it-yourself remodeling project.

We took off our shoes at the door and took turns at the washstand in the cramped family bathroom, as our hostess stood by holding a clean towel for us.

Raisa had made a grilled eggplant appetizer and *zharkoye*, a stew of potatoes, mushrooms, onions and meat baked in individual clay pots. She served it with a bottle of the local brew: 50-proof wine made from cranberries. (Vladimir was too far north for grapes to grow.)

"We had a celebration a number of years back of the 850th anniversary of the founding of Vladimir. Then they unearthed evidence that the city was even older than that, so we had to have another celebration a few years later."

After lunch, we all climbed in the blue Volga and Alexei drove us out to a church with a convent on the edge of town. It was a busy place. Three nuns in heavy black cotton work skirts were plastering the perimeter wall along the highway; the choir was singing inside the church. A relay of women parishioners in high heels and head scarves was taking a break from evening services to unload a truck, carrying sheets of wood paneling along with their handbags. A large garden of beets, cabbages, kohlrabi, squash and potatoes was growing beside the church. Behind it, fenced between the garden and the perimeter wall, a colony of chickens was clucking and scratching in the dirt. Workmen in canvas mitts were carrying bricks and scaffolding. Most of the nuns were young.

"The church is experiencing an upswing," said Alexei. "I think people are turning to it more now because their lives are more difficult."

Another tiny white Orthodox church, the Church of the Intercession, stood in the middle of an emerald green expanse of grass on the outskirts of Vladimir, several kilometers beyond the monastery. Alexei gamely guided the sedan down a steep hill and through bumps and potholes toward it until we came to the place where the dirt road passed under a railroad overpass. At the low point under the overpass, the road had become a large deep pond due to the recent rains. I talked Alexei out of attempting to ford it, and he gratefully eased the shiny blue car to a stop beside the road. He stayed behind to guard the car against bandits while the rest of us – Raisa and Yevgenia in high heels – climbed over the railroad tracks and set off on foot along the soft dirt road cutting through the green expanse.

We walked for an hour, passing a herd of milk cows with three nun-cowherds along the way and pausing for a rest break in a shallow ravine. Yevgenia began to lament that her shoulder bag was growing heavy; she had forgotten to remove the cucumbers that Raisa had given her at the apartment.

At last we reached the church grounds. The place was a paradigm of pastoral idyll, blissfully free of broken glass, litter and other attributes of civilization. The church itself, built in the year 1165, had a single onion dome [60] and Egyptian relief work along its three whitewashed masonry arches. Three monks sang in harmony inside. Beside the church, in a small pond edged with lily pads, a peasant in knee-high boots fished from a tiny boat. Cabbages, pumpkins, beets and potatoes grew in a black-earth garden out back.

---

60. The onion dome was added later. Twelfth Century Eastern Orthodox domes tended to be a more cap-like, Byzantine style.

CHAPTER 9

HEART TROUBLE IN PARADISE

We left the church and headed back along the dirt road. Yevgenia was losing steam. She began to breathe heavily. Halfway back, she said she felt worse. She swallowed several pills from her purse.

"It's the change in atmospheric pressure," suggested Raisa. Dark clouds were appearing on the horizon.

The pills did not help; Yevgenia continued to reel. No doubt the cranberry wine at lunchtime hadn't helped either. There was a peal of thunder in the distance.

Fortuitously, an elegant black *Volga* sedan and a small rusty *Lada* were approaching us from behind. Raisa let the *Volga* pass (possibly gangsters) and waved at the *Lada*. The driver shrugged helplessly and pointed at his travelling companions. A woman holding a tiny baby was sitting in the back seat, and the rest of the car was stuffed with a bassinet and other baby things. Raisa waved more frantically. The car stopped, Raisa flew into an explanation, and somehow the baby stuff was hurriedly cobbled together to make enough room for Yevgenia, and then even Raisa, to squeeze in. I was clearly not going to fit. I promised to come quickly on foot.

"No! Yevgenia might get worse while we're waiting for you," Raisa insisted.

Meanwhile, the black *Volga* had stopped to see what was going on. I caught up to it to explain the situation; but the back door was already opening for me to jump in. Behind the tinted windows were three stylishly dressed New Russians. They were travelling with the young family in the *Lada* and were returning from the church we had just visited, where they had gone to arrange for the baby's baptism. The *Volga* had a "big car ride" which easily handled the soft humps in the dirt road. We quickly reached the railroad overpass and forded the pond underneath.

"That's our car there." I pointed to Alexei's sedan.

"Good luck to you," they wished me as I jumped out. The *Lada*, fording the pond behind us, was up to its radiator in water.

I helped Yevgenia from the *Lada* into Alexei's car. Raisa began to rummage in the first aid kit.

"No more pills!" I ordered. "Where's the mineral water?"

Alexei carefully waded around the muck to the trunk and retrieved the water and cups, then began to drive even more aggressively than usual, flashing his headlights at pedestrians who were unwisely threatening to jaywalk. Somehow, through all the lurching and jolting, Yevgenia managed to get the cup to her lips. The water revived her and she sat up and smiled. We all cheered. A moment later she settled her head back heavily against the seat again and closed her eyes.

Raisa directed Alexei through a maze of city streets to a clinic. A locked iron gate blocked the entrance driveway, but there was a small opening for pedestrians. Yevgenia had revived enough to walk through it, and we looked around for the 'Reception' entrance. No clear signage. An ambulance was parked at a door in the middle of the back side of the building, so we tried that entrance, climbing the stairs to the first floor. (Handicapped entrances are almost unheard of in Russia.)

It was Saturday evening and no one was about. The corridor was dark and quiet. A large sign ordered us to talk in whispers. We walked up and down the corridor in both directions and found nothing but locked doors: 'Library,' 'Technical Services,' 'Operating Room.'

"We don't seem to be in the right place," said Yevgenia, who was walking on her own by now. We retraced our steps out to the driveway where the ambulance was parked and found a lone pedestrian.

"Where is 'Reception?'"

"Around the corner of the building to the left."

We found the sign at last, climbed the steps into the building again and hurried down the corridor. A young woman in a wool overcoat caught up with us.

"Excuse me, can I help you?"

"Yes, I'm not feeling well." Yevgenia began to describe her symptoms.

"I'm sorry, we can't help you here. We don't have a cardiologist."

"But you must have a doctor on duty."

"Yes, but he's a surgeon, not a cardiologist."

"Where is he?"

"There's no use asking him – he'll tell you the same thing. We cannot help you here."

"And what are you?"

"I'm a nurse. I just put on this overcoat because I was cold." She flashed open the overcoat to reveal a pale blue cotton hospital uniform, and simultaneously flashed an embarrassed smile.

"Can't *you* help me?"

"No. Look, even if we examined you and found there was something wrong, there's nothing we could do here. We don't have any medicines."

"Isn't this a hospital?"

"Not the kind you're thinking of. All we do here is surgery."

"Do you charge for your services? " [61]

"Surgery is free. If you want anesthesia, you have to pay for it."

"Don't you have medicines for your surgery patients?"

"No, they have to bring their own. Look, we can't help you. We don't have *an-y-thing* here." She enunciated each syllable, huddling tightly under the overcoat, arms folded.

"Never mind," Yevgenia muttered to us, turning to leave. "Just take me home and I'll call 'Skoroye Pomoshch.'"

"I respect doctors more than anything," Yevgenia had told me the day before. "They come to you, climbing dark staircases to your apartment when you are in need."

"Doctors in the United States don't make house calls any more."

"I guess that's one of the good things left over from Communism."

---

61. During Soviet times, all medical care was free. Now there is a patchwork of free and for-pay clinics.

PART V

THE VOLGA

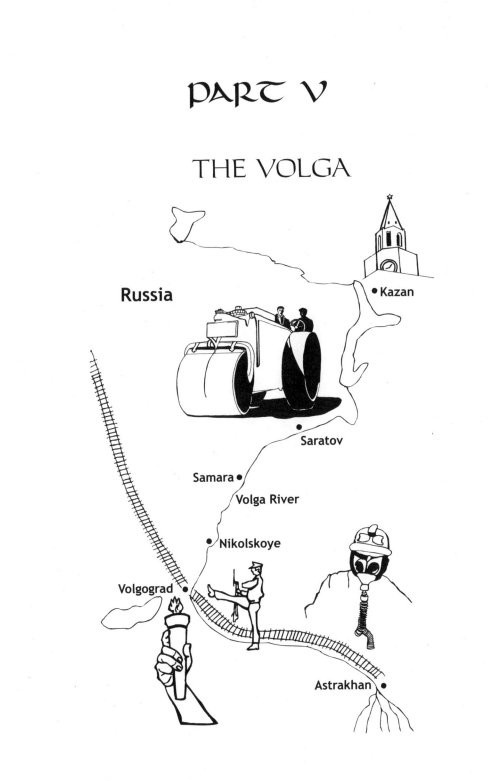

Stalingrad

The world knows Volgoyrad by its Communist-era name, Stalingrad. World War II put it on the map and into the history books for the 1942-1943 siege between the German fascists and the Russians over this strategic city where the Volga River links to the Don River through the Volga-Don Canal.

Chapter 1

Stalingrad

Volgograd, Russia, August 23.

It was the sixtieth anniversary of the Molotov-Ribbentrop Pact, in which Hitler and Stalin had designated spheres of influence in Poland, the Baltics and the Balkans. I paid a visit to Stalingrad's memorial hill, climbing many flights of stairs in the summer heat to reach a large, solemn reflecting pool. More than a million had died in the battle. 'A steel wind struck them in the face, but they all went forward...' read the inscription on a long gray wall beside the pool.

Two boys were splashing with delight in the cool dark waters of the reflecting pool. Soon, a guard in green fatigues appeared, obviously not pleased. He ordered the boys to follow him, carrying off their shoes as collateral to make sure they complied.

Higher up the hill, an eternal flame was guarded by stone-faced, goose-stepping young soldiers. All business while they were on duty, as soon as they had stamped noisily down the steps and around the corner, the young soldiers were happy to lend their weapons to a visiting heavy-metal gang for a photo op.

Chapter 2

Fire-Safe in Volgograd

The Hotel *Intourist* was graciously built, with high ceilings and a comfortable upstairs lounge. The price was the same for foreigners and Russian citizens. Hardly any Russians were about.

I climbed the wide staircase to the second floor and followed a rich red runner rug down the long parquet hallway to my room.

A diagram posted in the hallway directed me to a staircase on the right in case of fire, but the stairs were locked. I went back down to the desk to point out this contradiction.

"You'll have to talk to the director; I don't make the rules," said the administrator.

The director, Yevgeni Vasilievich, a slender, fifty-ish man wearing a crisply ironed short-sleeved shirt in the summer heat, had a desk in a quiet corner of the lobby with a small electric fan.

"The stairs are locked for your safety," he told me. "The times we live in are dangerous. What floor are you on?"

"The second."

"You really don't need the emergency stairs; you could get out through the window just fine from there."

"I don't think so."

"Come, I'll show you." He led the way from the lobby through the narrow entryway to the elevator bank and central staircase.[62] An old man stationed at the entryway greeted him with plantation manners.

---

62. Nearly all Soviet-built hotels are designed for strategic control of ingress and egress. Usually, the elevator and stairs are together in a choke point that can be watched by a single guard. If a hotel were ever to catch fire while full of guests there would be a severe bottleneck to get everyone out. The same problem occurs at many theaters and opera houses which, though well supplied with grand entry and exit doors, for some reason only allow one door to be opened when the event is over, forcing the entire audience to exit single file.

Once in my room, the director opened the casement window and stared at the breathtaking drop to the rooftop below.

"Yes, I guess it is a little far," he agreed. "But you must understand; we have a responsibility for the safety of our guests. We had a problem last year where one of the guests forgot to lock the door to their room and a stranger came up those stairs."

"Look, guests have a choice to lock their room doors. You've given me a key to my room. You have not given me any choice with respect to the emergency exit."

"If there is a fire, the floor lady has a key and will come and open it."

"Is the floor lady on duty all the time?"

"Yes."

He and I both knew it wasn't true. The floor duty desk near the main stairs had been empty when we passed, and the room keys were being given out at Reception.

"It's also not just," I continued, "for you to have a diagram in the hallway saying 'come this way, please – you will be able to exit here,' and then to have the way barred. You're putting people in *more* danger."

"Sometimes life is not just." [63]

"Is that your expectation – that life will not be just?"

He stared silently into the distance, seemingly lost in thought.

"No, life should be just," he said finally. "The stairs next to your room will be opened for the duration of your stay."

...and they *were*.

---

63. We were using the word *spravedlivii* for "just." It implies fairness and rightness in a sense completely separate from whether an act or situation is legal or illegal. Unlike the provisions of the new Constitution, the concept of fairness is widely recognized by ordinary Russians and deeply rooted in their culture.

Chapter 3

Evening with the Trendsetters

Volgograd, Russia, August 24.

The grand dining room on the second floor of the Hotel *Volgograd* had recently been re-born in a gracious style: high-ceilinged, with Corinthian columns, three enormous chandeliers, four tall arched windows on each side of the hall and a classical Greek frieze where the walls met the ceiling. All was flawless with fresh paint.

The tables were beautifully laid with crisp white linen. Candle-light shone through a plethora of polished crystal glasses and danced off sparkling sets of silverware and an array of china. Two mammoth bouquets of fresh flowers framed a small stage, over which a windswept Greek goddess presided in plaster relief.

But the tall wooden Art Noveau dining chairs were 97% empty, and management was taking steps to attract the moneyed set.

Since a great deal of the wealth in Russia today is made and con-trolled by muscle, the well-to-do tend to have different tastes from the upper class in other industrialized countries. Blue and gold bunting was draped over the flounced Soviet-style curtains. Rotat-ing colored disco lights, mirrored balls and bouquets of red, yellow and blue balloons were suspended from the high ceiling. Large black speakers mounted on the walls belted pop tunes.[64] In one corner was a bar selling stuffed animals. On the menu, along with the usual fare of sturgeon, *borscht*, cigarettes and alcohol, were prices for a number of more unusual items: picture-taking, fresh flowers, and

---

64. Russians enjoy popular music from around the world. Not only is American music widely played, but Russians have also written their own, drawing from many western styles as well as traditional Russian music. There is even a popular rock version of *Swan Lake*.

various pleasure services available right at the dinner table. There was even a list of prices for dismissing waitresses and other restaurant employees from work, though, in a world where some members of society are capable of spending in an evening what others earn in a year, it was unclear whether the price was for permanent firing with severance, or permission to go home early that evening. Most likely, it was payment for the waitress to spend the evening with her benefactor.

I had a bowl of Siberian-style *borscht*, then asked to try the Ukrainian style.

"It's the same soup," said the waitress, "only the Ukrainian borscht has fresh garlic added."

I puzzled over the price: the Ukrainian-style *borscht*, with its added ingredient, cost three roubles less than the Siberian. Was this another example of the topsy-turvy logic of the markets in the New East, or were diners willing to pay a premium for the privilege of having fresh breath for the duration of the evening?

A slick and suggestive cabaret dance show began as I left to catch my overnight train. Perhaps the big spenders knew what they were doing.

Chapter 4

A Hot, Dry Day

Astrakhan, Russia, August 25.

The night train clattered through the desert countryside at sunrise. Kilometers of dry, sandy scrub finally gave way to a verdant floodplain filled with small garden plots, where cabbages, potatoes and other northerly garden staples mingled with melon vines and apricot trees. In ancient times, the Caspian Sea had extended far north of Astrakhan, covering this floodplain. Now, the water level of the landlocked sea had dropped so much that one needed to travel a hundred kilometers downstream from Astrakhan to reach the famed lotus blossoms at the tip of the delta.

Strolling the streets of Astrakhan along with Slavic Russians were black-haired Turkic and East Asian citizens. Many of the slender Turkic women wore long, full, colorful skirts. Astrakhan was a crossroad, settled by, among others, Central Asian herders, German farmers and Jewish and Armenian traders.

The sun was already hot when the train pulled into town early in the morning. The handmade brooms used by the orange-vested station-sweepers were made from bushy sage-like pom-poms, rather than the straight "witch's broom" sticks used in their hand-made northern cousins.[65]

---

65. Manufactured brooms are virtually unknown in the former Soviet Union. Rather, brooms are hand fashioned by tying locally available twigs or straw to a wooden pole. Young military draftees ordered to sweep the sidewalks in front of their posts sometimes simply break branches from nearby trees to do the job. Snow shovels, too, are often hand made. On my street in the center of the capital city of Kiev, Ukraine, one of the residents assigned to daily sidewalk clearing duties had fashioned a snow shovel by attaching a handle to a heavy plywood board. Another had made a metal-edged snow pusher by fastening the blade of a crosscut saw upside down on the bottom edge of his wooden shovel.

A city bus waiting in front of the train station was already starting to fill up. I approached it.

"Lenin Square?"

Several locals nodded and motioned me on board. The driver went through the bus collecting coins.

What luck! There was one seat left – right up front. I carefully backed into it with my heavy pack (now provisioned for the culinary desert anticipated on the road east of Moscow.)

There was no "front door" on the bus. Rather, passengers boarded at the center of the bus and the entire space next to the driver was a steering-wheel-high carpeted expanse, littered with grimy spare bus parts, dishes of bolts, light bulbs and other odds and ends.

The bus grumbled down the city streets. As more passengers boarded along the route, coins were passed up the crowded aisle and I became the primary intermediary, passing them on to the driver and handing back tickets and change.

The bus took a turn to the left. Simultaneously, an old man sitting in mid-bus began to holler: "Driver, stop here!" The driver didn't hear him. "Stop!" he called again. "Lenin Square! *Zhenshina*,[66] get off!"

It was the old man who had advised me to get on. I squeezed through the crowded bus and onto the spacious street.

I found myself near the south wall of the *kremlin*, built after the Russian Czar Ivan the Terrible routed the Tatars from the city in 1556. The tall, whitewashed walls of the fortress were beginning to

---

66. *Zhenshina* means 'woman.' Now that Communism is falling out of favor, so is the Communist form of address, '*tovarishch*,' meaning 'comrade.' Instead, strangers on the street are addressed simply as 'man,' 'woman,' 'young man,' 'girl,' 'grandmother' (*babushka*) or 'daughter' (*doch* or *dochka* – used by older women toward a younger woman.) The term *devushka* (literally 'girl') has a much higher upper age limit than in the West. Nearly all female store clerks, regardless of age, are called 'girl,' and even middle-aged women on the street, particularly if they are slender and attractive, are often called 'girl.' The term 'boy,' on the other hand, fades out at a younger age and is replaced by 'young man,' except in endearing contexts equivalent with the English expression 'a night out with the boys.' It would never be used to gain the attention of a male shop clerk, for example.

peel badly in the bright sun. Behind the parapets, the green, cap-like domes of the early eighteenth century cathedral were topped with gold Eastern Orthodox crosses. Smaller chapels bore green onion domes. The gold crosses atop these domes were missing the lower, angled cross-piece typical of the Eastern Orthodox cross. In its place was a gold crescent with the tips of the crescent pointing skyward.[67]

As I walked down side streets toward the river, the aging facades of mid-rise apartment buildings gave way to ancient, picturesque, unpainted dark wooden one- and two-story homes with bright green and blue shutters. The wooden homes were typical of homes elsewhere in Russia, but the window frames and shutters – the only part of the exterior other than the door to know a coat of paint – were plain rather than intricately carved. Canna lilies and locust trees framed the cracked concrete paths of a small park, and cottonwood trees grew tall on the streets near the river.

---

67. I noticed similar crosses atop churches from Suzdal to Irkutsk, and received varying explanations of their symbolism. The most common explanation given by ethnic Russians was that the upturned half moon at the base of the cross symbolized Christianity's superiority over the Muslim religion of the Tatars.

CHAPTER 5

FULL BOAT GOING NORTH

Astrakhan, Russia, August 25.

The River Station Ticket Office was a green-and-white wooden gingerbread-trimmed building that had seen much better days. A large knot of people had assembled to try to buy tickets on the *Nekrasov*, a passenger ship from Moscow. It had arrived that morning and would be heading back up river in the evening.

I approached the knot of people. "Who's last?" The responses were ambiguous. Fingers pointed here and there.

I set my pack down and took up a position designed to intercept newcomers while giving those already waiting a turn ahead of me. One of the two ticket windows was open. The other window was blocked by a piece of wood, and the clerk behind it was busy having a conversation with someone inside. Half an hour passed. The line did not seem to be moving at all. At last, two pleased pensioners stepped away from the open window clutching tickets and the remains of the partially-clipped pages of their retiree benefit coupons.

A stylish blond woman in tight jeans and clunky heels stomped up to the line and elbowed her way toward the ticket counter. Noise erupted from all quarters of the crowd and a vicious, lengthy argument ensued as to whether the woman had properly followed the Byzantine rules of post-Soviet line protocol.

But the argument was for naught. The clerk stuck her head out the window to announce that the tickets on the *Nekrasov* were all sold out. The next passenger-line ship was due in two days, and any available space would not be sold until it arrived. Those who wanted a chance to buy a ticket could line up early in the morning.

No great loss. I was ready to pull off the road for a while and eager to soak up some sun after a long patch of rainy days farther north. I strolled up the quay to the *Lotus* Hotel.

CHAPTER 6

RED TAPE AND HEAVY ARMS
IN THE DEEP SOUTH

Astrakhan, Russia, August 25.

There seemed to be a lot of guns and uniforms hanging around the *Lotus* Hotel lobby. I approached the administrator.

"Any rooms available?"

"No. There might be some tonight but we won't know until this evening. Here is our telephone number. Call us after 8 p.m." She handed me a slip of paper.

One other hotel in town formally accepted foreigners. There was no room at that inn, either, but the nice proprietor called around and found that there was a room 'without conveniences' at the *Astrakhanskaya* Hotel.

The *Astrakhanskaya* was a turn-of-the-century brick building on a cottonwood tree-lined street between the river and the *Kremlin*. The administrator acknowledged that yes, indeed, she had a room, though it was available for one night only. She handed me two small brownish forms to fill out (in duplicate) with my name, address, passport data, residence, etc. The room was a double. I could either pay 105 roubles for one bed and share the room with a stranger of the administrator's choosing, or I could pay for both beds.

"I'll pay for both beds."

"That will be 210 roubles. May I have your passport please?"

I handed over the precious worn navy blue booklet and my visa.

Her expression changed. "Oh, you're a *foreigner*. That makes a difference."

"It doesn't make any difference." I began reaching into my briefcase for the ever-handy Russian Constitution.

"Yes it does make a difference. Just a moment. I have to ask whether I can let you stay here." She walked away with my documents and returned a few minutes later.

"Yes, you can stay, but the price will be double."

The Constitution was already falling open in my hands to Article 62. I pushed it under the window.

"You can't charge me double."

"Go talk to the director. First door to your left."

The director carefully scanned the section. "All right, you can have the citizen's price."

The administrator sat down with the forms I had filled out and began inking in the necessary documents: a thin brownish receipt, together with carbon copy, for my cash payment; a thin brownish slip to give to the floor lady in exchange for the room key, and a thin brownish slip to use as a breakfast chit in the morning.

Finally she handed me the whole stack. "May I keep your copy of the Constitution until the evening? I'd like to read that passage again."

"Of course you may," I said proudly, the thought of a soft bed in a private room also helping to make my pack feel light. "Could you stamp my visa, too, please?" I showed her what the other hotels had done. I knew I was asking a lot.

"Sorry, we don't have a stamp like that. You can try going to the Office of Visa and Registration this afternoon." She wrote the address on a slip of paper.

There was no elevator. I walked up two gracious but seemingly endless flights of stairs to the third floor, found the floor lady and followed her around the twists and turns of the hallway to my room. The emergency exit next to the room was padlocked. I was going to have to pick and choose my battles, and this one was not for today.

I freshened up at the sink in the communal bathroom. There did not seem to be any showers.

Russian women were washing plates of peppers and tomatoes in the bathroom sink as well. Many of the holiday-makers in the hotel were obviously "dining in," eating their fill of the ample fresh produce purchased from the late summer open air bazaars in town.

A large hollowed-out watermelon rind was parked in the hallway outside one of the rooms, leaking sticky pink juice onto the scuffed wooden floor. An aging cleaning lady in an enormous brown polka-dotted cotton dress and white head scarf muttered as she picked it up and dumped it into her heavy steel waste bucket.

Back outside on the street, the day was hot and dry. The Office of Visa and Registration (OVIR), which I had last dealt with (unsuccessfully) in Moscow, was closed until two o'clock, but the shade under the trees in the park was cool and deep. A trio of wiry peasant men with two axes, a cross-cut saw and a wooden push cart were cutting up a fallen tree into wood for one of the *shashlik* stands. I bought a copy of *Izvestia* and read the ongoing saga of *Kommersant*, the national business newspaper, whose office in Moscow had been sealed by the authorities a few days earlier due to 'fire code violations,' shutting down the presses. The paper seemed to be having a string of difficulties lately. In early August, it had printed the results of an incriminating audit of the Central Bank's use of International Monetary Fund monies, and shortly after that the editor had been dismissed.

The Coke vs. Pepsi cola wars were in full swing in the park, with their respective red and blue flags and posters far outstripping the advertising budget of any home-grown company. I tried the local cola brew instead, which tasted just like the other two.

I wasn't the only one in town buying locally-made products that day. On a leafy side street nearby was a busy grocery and delicatessen beneath a sign reading "Astrakhan Without America."

At OVIR, the guard at the door sent me to wait in the dark hallway outside Door Number 8 – 'Reception of Foreigners.' Most of the people waiting did not seem to be foreign.

Twenty minutes later it was my turn. The young man in uniform across the table looked like he would fit right into the Third Reich.

I explained the problem: OVIR in Moscow had told me that a hotel was required to register me, and yet here was one that couldn't, because it did not have a stamp. I of *course* wanted to be in full compliance with the law. Could he please stamp my visa?

"Not every hotel *should* have a stamp," he snapped back.[68] He took his time scrutinizing the existing stamps in my visa. This was his opportunity to find something I had done wrong; some flaw, some hook on which to hang me.

"What are you doing in Astrakhan?"

"I am here as a tourist." It was none of his damn business, but there was an imbalance of power here that would make such a smart answer fool-hardy.

"Come with me." He picked up my passport and visa, walked down the hall and dropped them on the desk of a colleague. "Come back for them on Friday." He said 'Friday' in English – his first and only English word.

It was Wednesday.

"I won't *be* here on Friday."

I'd be up a creek if my passport and visa stayed on that desk. The *Astrakhanskaya* Hotel was allegedly "full" for Thursday night. I would either need to find a hotel willing to accept me for the night, or buy a plane, train or boat ticket out of town, any one of which was going to require a passport, not to mention the fact that I would need my passport to travel onward if I did manage to buy such a ticket. I also needed to change money, which, without a passport, could only be done with the young men hanging around outside the money-changing booths. Not a good idea for half a dozen reasons.

"Well, we're closed tomorrow. Next time stay in the *Lotus* Hotel. If you want the registration issued today, you'll have to pay this sum

---

68. There was no direct evidence, but it seemed that someone was seeing to it that foreigners had limited hotel options in Astrakhan. In Soviet times, this practice facilitated keeping an eye on visitors and also steered foreigners to accommodations considered more presentable. Cynically, even today, when surveillance of foreigners is of much less interest to the authorities than money, it would be much easier for a local government kingpin to let hotels charge foreigners above-market prices – and perhaps skim a little for himself, by holding back the supply of rubber stamps and rigidly enforcing the registration requirement. Administrators in "locals only" hotels in Astrakhan seemed genuinely cowed – more so than anywhere else I visited in Russia – about letting a foreigner in.

for same-day service." He wrote an astronomical sum on a slip of paper and handed it to me.

"Do you mind telling me what the legal basis for that charge is?" The amount was a month's wages for many bureaucrats. "The visa registration fee is supposed to be 16 roubles."

"Sixteen roubles *and 80 kopecks*," he corrected me, getting hot under the collar. "Look, if you don't understand what you have to do, go get yourself an interpreter and then come back and talk to me."

"I can understand you just fine. Do you have a citation to a regulation or instruction on which the fee you're asking for is based?"

"Go get an interpreter. I don't want to talk with you any more."

He didn't mean 'interpreter'; he meant a facilitator who would grease the way. I picked up my passport – at least he had given me a cue to do so – and left, unregistered.[69]

The afternoon was sweltering. I ducked into a small shop to buy some mineral water. The clerk pulled a chilly one-and-a-half liter bottle from her refrigerator. I laid a well-worn bill on the well-worn counter. Next to us, on the same counter, was an unwrapped display of meat, covered with flies and darkening in the summer heat.

I stopped to weigh myself on a bathroom scale that an old woman had carried out to the sidewalk, and put a rouble in her hand. Fifty-seven kilos. The scale was probably frightfully inaccurate, but she owned her own business and I was supporting a private enterprise with no middlemen.

---

69. I couldn't help sympathizing with the Russian people just a little bit more after the encounter. I was definitely pushing the limits, banking on the fact that I would be leaving town, out of the jurisdiction of this petty bureaucrat with his custom-made rules and well-stuffed pockets. I had gotten away with shooting off my mouth – of demanding, with chutzpah, legal rights and legal citations. Most of the citizens around me were stuck in this isolated town, hemmed in by Kazakhstan, the Caspian Sea, the desert and, to the South, the explosive North Caucuses. Job promotions, school admissions and everyday life would be made difficult for them if they questioned bureaucratic caprice as I did. Their choices were to live as quietly as possible outside the law, forever vulnerable to prosecution or blackmail, or to pay sums for which there was no legal explanation in order to obtain obligatory stamps on an endless series of documents which served little useful purpose.

Wandering further down the street, I joined a crowd gathered around a table full of campaign T-shirts for right-wing presidential candidate Vladimir Zhirnovsky. The shirts were made very cheaply and selling for a ridiculously low price. The woman next to me confided, as she held one up for size, that she couldn't care less about the slogan, but for the price she might buy one to wear to bed.

Back at the *Astrakhanskaya* Hotel, evening life was setting in. Unlike the Intourist hotels I had stayed in, which were often nearly empty (too pricey for many to afford even at "citizen's" rates), the *Astrakhanskaya* was alive with people. In the sweltering evening air, hallway doors and windows were thrown open, revealing three, four, five and six-bed rooms, with unrelated occupants and entire families sitting semi-clad on rumpled sheets. A large group of children was playing boisterously in the hall. The floor lady interrupted her telephone call to shush them.

"We're leaving tomorrow," volunteered one of the sweaty, animated kids, smiling at her.

"And I'm counting the hours." She rolled her eyes.

"Is there a shower in this hotel?" I asked before she could return to her long conversation.

"No, unfortunately, but there's one in the courtyard. Come down tomorrow and I'll show you where."

I stopped by the front desk.

"Here's your Constitution back. Thank you."

"Can you tell me yet whether there will be any rooms available *tomorrow* night?"

"Sorry, the director has to give permission before I can let you stay another night. She'll be here in the morning." [70]

I walked back down the quay to the *Lotus* Hotel to try to hedge my lodging options for the next night. The breeze blowing across the river at sunset was refreshing. *Shashlik* sizzled at half a dozen

---

70. Like millions of ordinary Russians, I was now in the position of a supplicant. Bureaucratic discretion has been a time-honored way of life throughout Russian history. It has kept ordinary citizens meek and compliant. Gifts must be given, favor must be curried and mouths must be kept shut — all without the need for any commitment, on the part of the bureaucrat or clerk in power,

small private barbecue stands. There was a "floating swimming pool" complex in the river, consisting of a series of docks enclosing three claustrophobic-sized pools. A few meters farther down a woman was scrubbing and sudsing a carpet spread out on the cement embankment. In the water below, discarded plastic bottles and other junk floated in eddies of brown foam.

The *Lotus* Hotel resembled an armed camp. A score of polished official cars and police vans were parked out front. The steps leading to the hotel entrance were manned by a dozen armed men in various stages of uniform, camouflage, business suits and black T-shirts. One of the men, walkie-talkie in hand, stopped me.

"Excuse me, can you tell me where you're going?" He was polite and professional.

"Yes, I would like to ask the administrator whether she has any rooms available for tomorrow evening."

He smiled and let me pass. My foreign accent was undoubtedly an asset.

Inside the hotel lobby the atmosphere was silent, airless, and heavy with armed power. Well-built men with side-arms and Kalashnikovs were standing strategically every few meters, facing various directions. A particularly large group was sitting in armchairs around the entrance to the elevator bank and stairs like a pride of predatory cats waiting to spring. I walked slowly and carefully across the lobby, threading my way around them, visualizing myself stumbling over a shoelace and being flattened in a second.

A glow of perspiration stood on the administrator's forehead, along with a few wisps of hair that had come loose. Her eyes met mine, communicating a silent sigh of the stress she felt. It had obviously been an exhausting day. She still couldn't tell me whether there would be a free room the following night. I wanted to ask who

---

that doing so will be enough to garner even the smallest favor. Through much of my travels in the former Soviet Union it was impossible for me to experience life as it was for local citizens for, as soon as my nationality became known, the way was paved for me. Here, in isolated Astrakhan, the protective layers seemed to have been stripped away, replaced by unvarnished reality.

the important guest was, but was conscious of the many ears around me. Later, back in my room at the *Astrakhanskaya*, after pulling the long wires attached to the television rabbit ears to and fro and finally hanging them on the open window casement, I tuned in the evening news and learned that the city was hosting a meeting of the ministers of defense of the Commonwealth of Independent States countries. The first casualties of the new Chechen war, in Dagestan, a short distance to the south, were being flown to hospitals in Volgograd.

Astrakhan, Russia, August 26, 8:00 a.m., the Astrakhanskaya Hotel.

I turned in my breakfast chit for eggs and sausages cooked to order, sharing the *bufet* with just a handful of *biznesmen* and a blaring TV. Breakfast, it seemed, was optional and most of the guests had opted to save the extra dollar and breakfast in their rooms.

8:40 a.m., the Astrakhanskaya Front Desk.

The administrator still could not tell me whether I could stay another night.

"The director will be in by ten o'clock. I can't do anything without her approval."

I was eager to stay in Astrakhan another day, in the hope of booking passage on the *Gertsin*, a passenger ship due in the next morning. Finding an empty space on a train northward was going to be very difficult. The remaining families with children would be heading out in order to reach the cities in the North before the first day of school on September 1. In addition, I could be competing for space on the train with ethnic Russians fleeing from the Dagestan hostilities. I might very well wait in lines at the ticket windows all day long without success. Travelling further south to the next city, Makhachkala in Dagestan, was out of the question. Nor was I eager to fly, knowing nothing about the airworthiness of whatever puddle-jumper might be serving this backwater town, and knowing less about the military situation I might find at the airport in light of the defense ministers' conference and the nearby war.

9:00 a.m., Sperbank, the local savings bank.

"May I cash some traveler's checks?" My rouble supply was dwindling.

"Unfortunately not. We won't have any cash until 10:00 a.m."

It was already my second trip to the bank. The previous afternoon I had been told that traveler's checks were not accepted after 4:00 p.m., though the bank was open until 6:00.

10:00 a.m. the Astrakhanskaya Hotel.

A different administrator was on duty at the front desk, busily reading a magazine.

"May I pay for tonight now?"

"No, we won't know until after lunch whether we will have room."

"But don't I need to vacate my room by noon?"

"Well, then you'll just have to move out," she snapped.

"Where is your left luggage room?"

"We don't have one."

"But the sign on the second floor says that you do."

"No we don't; it's full."

I hurried across town to the "Government Administration of the Oblast" Hotel, a quiet, dimly-lit, nondescript building. A cleaning lady was folding linen in the lobby. She called the administrator to the desk.

The administrator was a slender, well-mannered soft-spoken woman of 60, who carefully listened as I told her who I was and what I needed.

I pulled out all the stops. For the first time since my encounter with Belarussian customs two months earlier, I laid my British Embassy ID card on the table.

Still, she hesitated. "Why aren't they letting you stay in the hotel where you are currently registered?" (Perhaps I was damaged goods and she should not get involved.)

"The *Astrakhanskaya* was pre-booked for tonight – there aren't any rooms left."

"Oh. I see." She paused. "Well, come this evening."

I immediately handed over my passport and visa. She did a double take.

"You want to register *now*?"

"Yes, I have to move my things by noon."

She paused again. "Well, OK, bring your things over. We can register you then."

I thanked her. I could already feel this room slipping out from under my feet like beach sand from a retreating ocean wave. Time to try the *Lotus* armed encampment again.

On the way back through the center of town, I stopped at the *Sperbank* again to try to change my traveler's checks. There were only two Roma men in line ahead of me, but after a forty-minute wait the line hadn't moved an inch. Whoever was in the booth ahead of us must have been changing enough money to pay off the national debt. I dashed back to the *Astrakhanskaya* to move out by the noon deadline.

12:30 p.m., the *Lotus* Hotel.

"Yes, we have a room available now."

With great relief I lowered my heavy pack to the floor.

The administrator, a new one since the night before, took my passport and visa and filled out the multitude of registration forms. The cashier next to her wrote out an invoice and handed it to me: 519 roubles.

"Excuse me, there seems to be a mistake. The price list posted on the wall says single rooms are 272 roubles."

"Yes, but you're a foreigner."

"But the Constitution says..." I laid the pamphlet on the counter.

The cashier chuckled malevolently. "That's *your* Constitution; this is ours." She tapped the registration documents and invoice with a firm finger.

"Oh, no," I continued with a straight face. "This is *your* Constitution." I showed her the cover of the booklet.

"Pfft! Go talk to the director." She pointed to a door at the end of the lobby.

I knocked on the door.

"Come in, sit down," said a well made-up woman with soft, full cheeks, a faint smell of perfume and an ample frame. "What is the problem?" she asked graciously.

"I'm trying to rent a room here…"

"We don't have any rooms available."

"Yes, you do. The administrator has already registered me and the cashier has written up the invoice. The only problem is that the price I am being charged is higher than that posted on the wall."

The director pressed a button on her speaker phone. "Would you come in here please?"

A moment later the administrator appeared.

"Did you promise this woman a room?"

I held my breath and listened to my heart pounding in my ears.

"Yes."

I breathed again.

"How is it that we are registering people without a *zayavka*?"

A discussion followed as to how an extra room had been identified. The administrator left and the director turned back to me.

"The reason you are being asked to pay more is that we are giving you a *better room*. We have a special floor just for foreigners. The rooms have entirely different accommodations – different sheets, different towels, different television sets…"

"I'm not asking to be treated specially. I'm asking for the same conditions given to citizens."

"Sorry, we don't have any "citizen's" rooms available until the 28th. We *do* obey the law. This is a private hotel and we are free to set our own prices."

"Yes, of course, but the prices and conditions must be the same for foreigners and citizens."

I was going to lose this argument. The public accommodations in this muggy river delta city, it seemed, had taken a page from the Louisiana law books of the 1890's: separate and unequal was the highest law of this land, and I would be sleeping on the street if I made further issue of it. I didn't have enough roubles to pay the inflated foreigners' price, but obtained dispensation to leave my heavy pack behind the desk while I hiked across town to the *Sperbank* again.

1:20 p.m. *Sperbank.*

The security guard met me in the entry and barred the way. Closed. It was lunch hour. The bank would reopen at 2:00.

I waited. One of the employees was obviously having a birthday, for bunches of flowers and well-wishers kept appearing at the door.

2:10 p.m. Sperbank.

The lunchtime festivities were finally over and the bank reopened. I was first in line for foreign exchange. I entered the booth and closed the door behind me. The exchange clerk was sitting at her desk, but a small sign was tacked up: "ten-minute break." It seemed that there was a computer problem; a technician was looking over her shoulder.

The ten-minute break stretched to 25 minutes. At last she was ready to help me, and yes, she could cash travelers' checks. I countersigned several and shoved them through the drawer under the bullet-proof window, along with my passport. She got out a magnifying glass on a little stand and examined the checks, front and back, first under a bright light, then under an ultraviolet light, then under the bright light again. At last she was satisfied that they were not counterfeit, and began entering the transaction in her computer. Alas, it was down again. The technician was called back in.

An hour later I was out on the street again. I made my way back to the Lotus Hotel, laid the cash down on the cashier's desk, gently retrieved my pack and tiptoed across the lobby and through the gauntlet of muscled men at the elevator bank. The men shrank back chivalrously to allow me through.

The elevator whined upward, then halted with a lurch at the Foreigners' Only Floor. On the landing, an outgoing young Georgian soldier sat on guard duty. His Kalashnikov rested comfortably on the sofa next to him. Upon hearing my nationality, he brightened and conveyed his good wishes to America. The floor lady cheerfully handed over my key. With great relief, I unlocked a room with a commanding view over the river, peeled off my sticky clothes, stood under the cold shower, and dried off with one of the special, thick Turkish "foreigners only" towels.[71] Accomplishments of the day as of 3:30 p.m.:

1. Changed money;
2. Settled into hotel.

---

71. Hotel towels generally consist of a small terry-cloth towel and two "dishtowels:" one of cotton waffle weave for scrubbing and one, of starched linen, that is completely non-absorbent.

CHAPTER 7

UP THE VOLGA RIVER

Astrakhan, Russia, August 27, 6:00 p.m.

A flotilla of three passenger ships pulled out of the Astrakhan River Port. Fuzzy speakers on the cruise ship ahead of us were belting out a rousing Souza-esque march tune. I went to the Key Room to rent some sheets from the *provodnitsa*.

"Are those keys hanging behind you to empty cabins? There's a bad smell in Cabin 120."

I really shouldn't be complaining too loudly; I had been fortunate enough not only to obtain a place on the *Gertsin*, but also to secure a double cabin in which the second bunk had gone unsold. Passage on the five-day cruise from Astrakhan to Kazan was 519 roubles (about $21), meals not included. In addition to two bunks, the cabin had a sink with hot and cold running water, a mirror, a wardrobe, a small table with a straight-backed chair and two portholes. Rolled up on top of the wardrobe were two life preservers made from heavy wooden slats sewn into orange canvas. They looked like they had been rescued from the Titanic, but were stenciled with a 1986 date of manufacture. There was no electric outlet in the cabin, and the cord on my laptop was not quite long enough to reach from the socket in the hallway to the desk.

"I can't make any cabin changes; I'm just the *provodnitsa*. But you can go up to the bridge and ask Nikolai Ivanovich. If he says it's OK, then anything is possible." [72]

---

72. In many former Soviet organizations, power is still concentrated at the top. High-level people are often looked to for even the most mundane decisions, because lower-level people are afraid of overstepping their authority, or simply don't know what to do. They are safer doing nothing than taking the

"Can you see if there are any single cabins available?"

Two of the ladies went off to find out.

"A single will be available when we get to Volgograd. In the meantime, all that's available is the *lux*. It's three thousand roubles."

I could easily afford it, but would certainly call a lot of attention to myself by pulling out such a wad of cash in a place where eating an ice cream bar in public could be viewed as conspicuous consumption by some. If I took the *lux* I would spend in five days what the ladies I was speaking with earned in a year. Plus, the *lux* had windows opening onto the public deck, which would mean keeping the curtains drawn or living in a fishbowl. I decided I'd rather leave the porthole open below for some fresh air and look out over the river.

"I'll take the single when we get to Volgograd."

4:50 a.m. Dark along the Volga; the full moon left a shining path along the water. Tiny waves from the boat's wake lapped gently a few feet below the open porthole.

The sound of a motorboat droned outside. I stuck my head out. A small boat was coming alongside, racing its motor to keep up with the larger ship. A dark figure seemed to be clinging to the ship.

"*Davai, davai!*" [73] called a male voice.

A robbery? It would be easy enough for a slender young man to drop in on sleeping vacationers enjoying fresh air for the night, then return to a motorboat and disappear among the willow trees and reeds along the bank. I slammed the porthole shut.

Soon the smell emanating from the sink drain became overpowering and I opened the porthole again. The motorboat was gone and the sky was beginning to pale. Layered sand cliffs appeared along the shore.

---

chance that they might do the wrong thing. This practice tends to slow down responsiveness to the needs of the "market."

73. This expression has various translations: 'come on,' 'go ahead,' 'go away,' 'let's go.'

CHAPTER 8

THE VOLGA BOATMEN-
TURNED-ENTREPRENEURS

Nikolskoye, the Volga River, Russia, August 28.

The *Gertsin* pulled into dock at a farming and fishing village for a "breakfast stop." The locals were waiting with piles of watermelons, *dinya* (a honeydew-like melon), eggplant, peppers, red tomatoes, hard green tomatoes, striped tomatoes, tiny purple grapes, apples, plums, rolls of fruit leather, dried fish, pickled fish in glass jars, eggs, milk fresh from the cow in plastic soda bottles and long curving slender green squash more than a meter in length. Irrigation water drawn from the Volga made this cornucopia possible, and the lotus land of the Caspian delta ever more distant.

"*Cherepakha!*" called an elderly woman wearing a headscarf, holding up a turtle in one hand. The turtle waved its legs helplessly in the air. "The meat is very tasty."

There were farmers with angular Central Asian faces, round Far Eastern faces, and Slavic Russian faces wrinkled by the strong southern sun. Cows ambled around freely behind the market stalls, gobbling up melon rinds and spoiled pieces of fruit tossed out by the marketeers. Pungent desert weeds lined the bottoms of lumbering watermelon trucks, cushioning the cargo. Rusty brown steel storage boxes the size of outhouses, some square, some hand made from a single cylinder of pipe, stood along the bank, and numerous rowboats were pulled up on the sandy shore. Nearby, a barge-and-tugboat combination was ferrying two cars across the river. The tug had probably been at work early to bring the melon trucks to the market.

Vacationers and petty traders from the ship slogged back and forth across the gangplank with buckets of yellow peppers under their arms and heavy sacks of watermelons slung over their shoulders, pausing to wipe their feet on the damp mop carefully left in the pathway for that purpose by the cleaning ladies.

The piles of fruit on board grew and grew. It seemed that if the boat stayed in port long enough, the entire inventory of the market would seep into the cabins, the hallways and the lounges.

The most intense activity was in the "crew only" area of the lower deck, near the engine room. Small motorboats moored along the side of the passenger ship and half a dozen young men formed a "watermelon brigade," passing the striped green fruit from the motorboats onto the open lower deck.

At 10:30 a.m. a deep horn sounded, the public address system crackled, and the ship pulled out into the river again. The passengers disappeared into their cabins to breakfast on their purchases, popping into the hallway now and then to heat water in small electric teapots at the 220-volt sockets in the hallway. The crew went to work storing its unofficial cargo, packing it into old wooden crates in the hold and filling one of the passenger lounges.

Viktor, a short, pudgy, elderly doctor from Saratov, came down to share some of my watermelon.

"How did you sleep?"

"I woke up at five. There was a motorboat alongside the ship."

"Ah, yes. I was up too then. We were passing the place that has red sturgeon, and the motorboats were offering it for sale. I wanted to buy some, but it was too expensive. They wanted a thousand roubles for some of the big fish — 45 roubles a kilo. The boys on the crew bought some; they have a tank in the hold where they can keep the fish alive until they get to Moscow in nine days. If you're an ordinary passenger, they just throw the fish through your porthole."

The sturgeon riding in the hold tank were probably among a precious few that would make it past the upstream locks and dams alive.

CHAPTER 9

THE VOLGA SEWER

As Viktor and I talked the pile of watermelon rinds on the tiny cabin table grew and grew.

"Throw them out the porthole," Viktor instructed. "All the waste on this ship – on all the ships coming through here – goes into the river. The waste from the oil refineries upstream? Straight into the river! The sewage from all the cities we are passing? Into the river!"

"Untreated?"

"Yes."

"Aren't there laws against that?"

"Yes, but no legal action is ever taken. They always say 'we don't have any money to fix that' or 'no one is willing to work on that project.' All of it ends up in Astrakhan. Astrakhan is a dirty city. The people are sick: cholera; cancer. It has one of the highest mortality rates in Russia. People are drinking the water from the river because there is no ground water." [74]

Drinking Water

In many parts of the former Soviet Union, tap water is not drinkable for health reasons. Many Russians buy bottled water, often at a steep expense relative to their income. Others fill bottles at hillside springs to carry home for drinking. Russians drink a lot of tea and some boil water for drinking. While boiled water may have been a healthful choice in previous generations because the boiling killed microorganisms, it may not be adequate today in areas of heavy industrial pollutants, the extent of which is often unknown to consumers or perhaps even intentionally understated by local authorities and industries.

---

74. See sidebar *Drinking Water*.

The discussion turned to politics. "I don't read the newspaper any more. And I don't vote. It doesn't do any good. The politicians are buying votes. They come around and say 'vote for me and I'll buy you a beer.' People take them up on it because they figure it's a waste of time to vote, so why not throw it away."

Viktor asked if I could invite him to immigrate to the United States. It was a frequent request. Television had no doubt helped to give Russians the perception that life was substantially better in the United States.

Chapter 10

River Life in the Southern Desert

We spent the day soaking up the late summer sun on deck, and on a sandy beach during a recreational "green stop." The passengers from the cruise ships in our flotilla halted on the same beach, and entertained us all with a home-grown costume play. *Shashlik* sizzled on a barbecue grill hidden from the hot sun beneath a camouflage canopy of Soviet army origins.

Toward evening, the ship pulled into Akhtubinsk, another village along the riverbank. Elderly local women in cotton dresses, strong and wrinkled from years of farm work in the hot sun, were waiting with their fresh produce, neatly lined up along the pathway between the river dock and the village above. There were several beige brick stores in the village, and the cruise-niks traipsed in and out of them, looking for ice cream and candy.

One store was bypassed by all: the one with a fading hand-lettered sign above the door designating it as Store Number 3, selling agricultural products from the Vladimirskoye Collective Farm.[75] A dour woman sat silently behind a counter in the dark dusty room, hands folded. Caged up behind a metal grate on the other side of the room, untouchable, were plump watermelons and crates of eggplant, a relic of the days before the English word '*marketing*' crept into the Russian vocabulary.

A barge went by, piled with a brownish sand-like cargo.

"That's salt," said Volodya, a passenger who had joined us at Akhtubinsk. "There is a dried-up lake near here where it is collected."

---

75. See sidebar *Collective Farms*, page 148.

Night fell and the golden moon rose again. I slept on the top bunk, eye level with the open porthole, listening to the low hum of the ship's engine as it made its way steadily upstream in the gentle current. In the midnight hours, the engine dropped an octave and the ship slowed considerably. I heard the captain's voice on the public address system. The captain was a kind, steady, grandfatherly man with a ready smile. I had heard his voice many times during the voyage, making announcements. Now he was calmly giving instructions to the crew, for the river was shallow here. The hull beneath the floor of my cabin gently scraped a sand bar. I drifted back to sleep.

Collective Farms

Peasant farmers were forcibly collectivized in the new Soviet Union be-ginning in the late 1920's. This and Stalin's grain confiscation triggered a famine in Ukraine in the early 1930's that killed seven million. An-other round of collectivization occurred in the Baltics in the late 1940's, after their forcible annexation into the Soviet Union in World War II.

Often, several villages were gathered together under the umbrella of a single collective farm, which might range in size from about 1000 hectares (2500 acres) all the way up to 10,000 hectares (25,000 acres). Most collective farms are around 3,000 hectares.

Collective farm work is much more labor-intensive than farming in the West, and it is not uncommon for a 3,000-hectare farm to employ 500 or more workers. Most collective farms are diversified, producing a combination of grain, oilseed (such as sunflower), sugar beets, vegetables and fruit, along with sheep, poultry, cattle and dairy. (Crops vary de-pending on the climate where the farm is located.) Many farms conduct related operations such as milling, baking and transportation. Farms often produce the hay for their own animals, piling it up for storage into enormous stacks the size of football fields.

Now that the Soviet Union has broken up and privatization pro-grams developed, collective farm members in some of the newly independent states are permitted to take a share of the land and set up their own farming operations. Privatization is progressing rapidly in the Baltics and more slowly in other places. In Ukraine, even though some farm workers have not received their wages for several years, many have chosen to remain members of their collective farms. Factors con-tributing to this include inertia, lack of understanding of their legal rights, lack of experience in running a business, and, more fundamen-tally, the difficulties of making it alone as an independent farmer in a land where agricultural credit is essentially unavailable, reliable mar-ket information is difficult to obtain, the transportation and supply infrastructure is not set up to serve independent farmers, and access to social services such as schools and medical care may be available only through continued membership in the collective farm. Some find it more expedient to remain nominally a member of the farm while utilizing farm resources for private farming activities.

CHAPTER 11

HOW THE FIRST STEWARD LINES HIS POCKETS

Volgograd, Russia, August 29.

The ship pulled into the dock at Volgograd for a stop of several hours. As the passengers were de-barking to stretch their legs in town, a panel truck from a nearby farm pulled alongside on the quay. The back of the van was piled high with sacks of onions. Crew members hoisted the sacks up the gangplank to the ship and stored them in the passenger lounge along with the watermelons. These, too, would help supplement the crew's wages when sold up-river for a higher price.

"*Now* may I move to the single cabin?" I asked the *provodnitsa*. I might find myself with a strange cabin-mate at any moment if the second bunk in my existing cabin were sold.

"Ask Nikolai Ivanovich." A cleaning lady went to fetch him.

Moments later a tall, lumbering middle-aged man appeared, smoothing long strands of greasy gray hair over a large bald spot. Gaps of undershirt were visible between the lower buttons of his yellow uniform shirt, where his belly protruded well over the beltline.

"I'd like to take the single cabin now."

"It's only available until Saratov," he answered. We would be there in 24 hours. "What cabin are you in now?"

I told him.

"We will resolve the issue of changing your quarters after the ship leaves port today."

I stared at him silently.

"Do you understand?"

"Yes."

I understood completely. I went to the on-shore ticket office and bought out the second bunk of my existing cabin. [76]

High steep embankments lined with cement slabs appeared along the shore of the river. Close to the water's edge, people were sudsing carpets. Higher up, an old woman was grazing several goats on the weeds sprouting up through the cracks between the cement slabs. This was the entrance to Lock 31 – the first above the Caspian Sea. Our flotilla of two cruise ships and a passenger ship huddled into the lock together, and there was room for a fourth. A young couple from Moscow, not losing a moment's tanning time, stood with their backs to the hot sun, watching the side of the ship instead of the procedure at the locks.

---

76. The *Gertsin* was part of the state-owned "River Fleet." In a time-honored low-tech fashion, when the ship docked in port, the local ticket office would be told which bunks were available, tickets to those bunks would be sold to vacationers elbowing at the ticket window, and the fares paid would disappear into the behemoth state bureaucracy. If the ship left port with the single cabin still empty, I would be dealing with the First Steward directly. The difference I paid to upgrade would be handled off the books – and find its way into the First Steward's pocket. When we arrived in the next town with a ticket office he would again have to report the cabin as empty or else account for the fare, which explained his statement that the cabin was only available until we reached Saratov, even though there was no advance reservation system. In this manner, throughout the country, money-losing state enterprises with low-salaried employees stay in business.

CHAPTER 12

RAINY DAYS ON THE RIVER

The Volga River between Saratov and Samara, Russia, August 31.

During the night the clouds moved in. A faint drizzle was falling as the ship pulled into a sandy beach for another "green stop." Now the desert was gone and the shore was thick with trees. On the grassland bluff above the river a lone herdsman grazed a hundred horses. Up a muddy road was a village with a single paved street lined with a mixture of ancient sagging wooden houses and solid new brick ones, some still half-constructed. Chickens and geese roamed freely while the watchdogs were tied up. Cows grazed here and there. A water main ran parallel to the street, with spigots sprouting up perpendicularly here and there. Many of the homes were not connected to the water main. Old women with wooden yokes over their shoulders were carrying pairs of galvanized buckets full of water back to their homes. Behind the village was an abandoned dairy, no doubt part of a former collective farm.

Back on the ship it was cold and windy. Time to move indoors. The East Germans who had built the ship in Weimar in 1958 had provided for some gracious indoor living spaces. On one end of the mid-deck was a wood-paneled reading room with inlaid wood chess tables and a semi-circle of windows facing the river. On the opposite end of the ship was a music room with a piano.

The children on board had commandeered the reading room with its fuzzy television set, but in the music room there was only a fat woman with her daughter. I plopped down on the sofa, conveniently located next to the electric socket, to do some writing on the laptop. The fat lady looked up.

"Mumu scampered under the sofa a little while ago. Don't be afraid if she jumps out."

I moved to another chair across the room. There was a rodent-sized space between the sofa and the floor. Who on earth was 'Mumu?' There were several little dogs on board ship, and a few turtles had joined us at Nikolskoye. The place was beginning to look more and more like Noah's Ark.

Mumu did not respond to coaxing or being hollered at in Russian, so her owner disappeared, returned with a long stick, got down on her knees and began prodding, then groping under the couch. Mumu turned out to be a Siamese cat.

The Volga River, between Samara and Kazan, Russia, September 1.

It was my last day on the cruise. Not only rain, but also rough seas pounded the ship as it made its way across the gigantic Samarskoye Reservoir. I closed the porthole, leaving only a tiny crack open for some fresh air. It turned out to be too much. A wave crashed against the ship, soaking me and my breakfast and leaving a layer of water on the floor of the cabin. One of the cleaning ladies lent me a rag to mop up with. We were friends by now — several of them wanted to go to America.

"We make 700 roubles a month," they told me. "The ship works three months out of the year, and we get room and board then, too. The rest of the year we are unemployed. It's almost impossible to find another job."

At the end of the day we docked in Kazan. I turned in my sheets and towel to the *provodnitsa*, received my torn ticket stubs back, and walked off into the Kazan evening.

Chapter 13

Tatarstan

Kazan, Republic of Tatarstan, Russia, September 2.

Kazan. The city name sounded like it belonged to another time and place – Arabian Nights perhaps. But the Turkic people who once ruled over ancient Russia now had an island of semi-sovereign territory – the Republic of Tatarstan – in the green fields and forests of central Russia. Kazan, with as many minarets as onion domes, was its capital. *Zharkoye* clay pot stew was a popular dish, and tea was served with a slice of lemon and a dried apricot in the bottom of the cup for flavoring.

I wanted to check my e-mail. The flagship Intourist hotel I was staying in had no *biznes tsenter*, so I found the main Telephone and Telegraph Office and began reading the posted notices.[77] There was a telephone number for a service advertising hookup to the Internet from one's home computer.

I bought a *zheton* for the local call.

"Unfortunately," said the desk clerk, ringing up the tiny purchase and handing me a sales slip and the pleated metal disc to drop in the telephone, "local calls cannot be made here at the telephone

---

77. Every city has Telephone and Telegraph offices, rows of booths where citizens can make inter-city and international calls. Some of the telephones work with *zhetoni* (metal discs which are a different size and shape in each town), some work with microchip-embedded telephone cards, and some through an advance deposit given to the operator on duty. For a small additional fee, the operator can also "place" the call if one has trouble getting through by dialing it oneself. Some Telephone and Telegraph offices offer Internet access, either themselves or through a private business renting space in the building. In addition, private Internet services in town sometimes advertise on a bulletin board in the T&T office.

company – only from telephone booths on the street. There's one over there." She pointed across the street.

I crossed the street, waited in line at the booth and dialed the number.

"I don't know of any Internet cafes," said a young man on the other end of the phone, "but I'll ask around. Call me back in ten minutes."

I bought another *zheton*; the telephone ate it. I tried again and got through to the same young man. His name was Ainor.

"I didn't find any Internet cafés, but you can come over here and use the Internet." He gave me complex directions across town. "When you get to Building 54, ask the *dezhurnaya* at the entrance to call upstairs for me."

Half an hour later, with the help of a lot of nice people on the street,[78] I found Building 54. The *dezhurnaya* was sitting in a glass booth in the drafty entry hall.

I hollered through the glass. "Can you call upstairs and tell Ainor that I'm here?"

"Sorry, I can't hear you, come inside."

She opened the door to the booth. An overpowering smell of onions filled the air. Neatly laid out on paper towels on her desk were small heaps of sliced green onions and chopped dill. It was just lunchtime and colleagues were obviously expected shortly with hot soup.

A few minutes later Ainor appeared, wearing thick glasses and a short-sleeved white shirt with a pen in the pocket. He led the way upstairs and through a dark cavernous hall filled with tangles of wire and rows and rows of colored lights and gray metal boxes covered with loudly clicking switches. It was the telephone building, *sans* fiber optics. Ainor and two other nerds had a small glass office in the back with three computers.

---

78. Russians are very outgoing in both asking for and helping with directions on the street. I found that it helped to approach two or more people standing and chatting together, since they were more likely to be in their own neighborhood, not in a hurry, and in a mood to socialize. People walking dogs were also a good bet.

For an hour, I was connected to the modern world, then Ainor led me back through the pre-microchip maze.

"May I pay you for the use of the Internet?"

"Sure!" he said, his eyes lighting up as I handed him a banknote.

CHAPTER 14

A LENINIST
TRUE BELIEVER

The Lenin House museum in Kazan was not in the guidebook. I happened by 15 minutes before closing time. The door to the displays was already closed and the lights turned off, but when I stepped into the entrance hall, an energetic and indefatigably cheerful museum director greeted me. The display doors were immediately flung open and the red carpet rolled out. I felt like I was the first visitor in a week.

The prim, petite museum director delivered the tour personally. She was an unabashed Communist and wore it proudly.

"Communism is where you think about what the *other* person needs first, and *then* think about yourself. It worked quite well right after the Great Patriotic War. 'So many suits are needed in this city this year; if you please, here they are.' And the suits *always arrived.*"

"Then people started wanting to have *lots* of suits, or suits in different *colors,*" she continued. Her earrings, little white balls on tiny gold chains, swung fashionably as she bobbed her head about for emphasis. "They started thinking about *themselves* first. That's why we are having so many problems in Russia today: Capitalist ideas have taken hold. Capitalists only think about gathering as much as they can for themselves, and now there's not enough to go around."

The Ulyanov[79] family had lived in the house while Lenin was studying at Kazan University. He was there only briefly but, as everywhere else in Russia, every piece of furniture he might have touched was still carefully preserved and revered. To True Believers

---

79. Lenin's original last name. 'Lenin' was a Revolutionary pseudonym, as was 'Stalin.'

such as the woman in my presence, he personified a fusion of George Washington, Jesus Christ and Elvis Presley.

Her chic high heels clipped gracefully down the narrow wooden stairs to the museum office, while I padded behind wearing *tapochki,* clinging to the steep railing.

"Would you sign our guest book please? And also I need to charge you the museum entry fee. That will be 3 roubles. *Before,* all the museums were *free.*"

A Vast Northerly Continent

The territory of Russia is, in a way, a stretched mirror image of North America. Most of the old European-style cities are in the West, while Vladivostok – like San Francisco or Victoria on the opposite shore – stands vigil over the Pacific. In between, rolling, virtually empty countryside filled with birch trees, hayfields, great lakes, steppe and mountain ranges is interspersed with ugly, sprawling cities that grew there in the process of exploiting the abundant natural resources. For a fair comparison of the size of Russia, one must think of the United States and Canada combined. The distance from Moscow to Vladivostok is twice that from New York to San Francisco, and the Trans-Siberian railroad traverses a latitude equivalent to that of central Canada. Without a network of highways, the railroad is the only reliable way to cross the eastern territory by land. In many small towns, the daily trains are the lifeblood of the local economy, bringing out dozens of villagers with small carts, buckets and tiny folding tables bearing garden plot produce and home-cooked food. Those who have scraped together a little start-up capital practice the art of capitalism, buying a few cartons of packaged snack foods or soft drinks from a trader on one train and selling items individually to passengers on the next train for a markup.

PART VI

THE TRANS-SIBERIAN RAILROAD - WEST

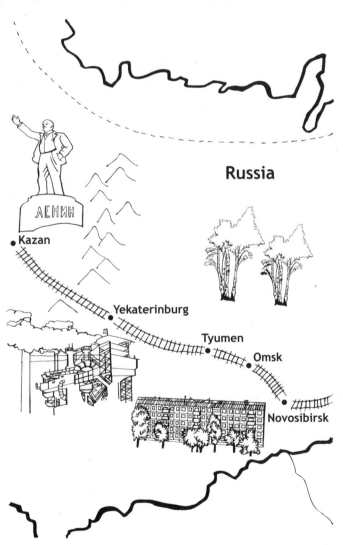

Russia

Kazan

ЛЕНИН

Yekaterinburg

Tyumen

Omsk

Novosibirsk

Chapter 1

The Urals

Yekaterinburg, Russia, September 3.

The mining-oriented metropolis of Yekaterinburg, just east of the Ural Mountains, still answered to its Soviet-era name, Sverdlovsk, in most parts of town. Breakfast at the *bufet* of the Hotel *Sverdlovsk* was a coronary delight: two boiled wieners, two slices of cheese, two slices of butter as large as the cheese slices, a single round white roll and a cup of tea, sweetened to the taste of the round matron whose job it was to walk the plate across the room.

While Stalin might have carted everything of value east of the Urals to keep it out of the hands of the invading Nazis, he seemed to have carted everything of any cultural value back to Moscow and Leningrad when the war was over. A few giant rock-breaking hammers and an old Bessemer Converter stood in the yard of the Architecture and Industrial Technology Museum. The interior displayed student models of handsome but as yet unbuilt buildings. To fill the shelves of the History and Local Studies Museum, it appeared that a group of grocery store window decorators has been given boxes of books left behind by fleeing bourgeoisie (or murdered Romanovs[80]) and told to arrange a display. The eclectic array was augmented with photos, medals and text honoring the city's *Stakhanovtsi*, those who, during Communism, knocked themselves out to overfill their work quota by a thousand percent or more.

Getting out of Yekaterinburg was a truly Soviet experience. Fresh off the train from Kazan, I got in line to buy the next ticket onward, to Novosibirsk, carefully choosing the trains through Tyumen rather

---

80.   The Czar and his family were executed in Sverdlovsk in 1918, bringing the
      Romanov family dynasty to an end.

160

than Petropavlovsk. Trains to the latter city would cross through a corner of Kazakhstan, possibly causing a raft of visa problems.

"You can't buy a ticket now. Try tomorrow after 9:30 a.m."

It turned out that those originating their journeys at the train's starting point (often Moscow) had a preemptive right to buy tickets. I would have to wait until the train left its city of origin to purchase an unsold ticket.

I returned to the train station the following morning and waited in line at one of the ticket windows.

"Do you have any tickets to Novosibirsk yet?"

"No."

"When will you know?"

"I don't know."

"When should I ask again?"

"You can ask any time you like."

I got in line at a different ticket window and asked again.

"I don't know when we will receive word. Go ask *Spravochnoye*."[81]

I got in line at *Spravochnoye*.

"There's one ticket left on the midnight train to Novosibirsk, in *Lux*. Train number 110."

I thanked her, raced back to a ticket booth and waited in line again.

"Sorry, I don't find *any* tickets at all available on that train."

"But *Spravochnoye* just told me…"

"It must have been sold while you were waiting in line. Oh, but here's a place in *Platzkarte* on the 3:51 a.m. train."

"I'll take it."

---

81. There is a high division of labor in Russian train stations. Some clerks sell tickets just for war veterans and invalids, some just for children, and some, with the longest lines, to everyone else. There are sometimes special booths serving foreigners, but these are not always in the main ticket hall. Those who sell tickets do not give out information. Departure and arrival times, ticket costs and other details must be obtained from the 'Information' booth, *Spravochnoye*, which does not sell tickets.

Vladimir Putin's Rise to Power

As I made my way eastward, I bought newspapers and other provisions at the kiosks lining the train platforms, and stopped for a few days at a time in towns along the way. The news was filled with reports of apartment buildings in the Russian heartland blowing up in the night. It was reported that sugar sacks filled with explosives and fitted with primitive timing devices had been carried into the basements of grocery stores located on the ground floors of the apartment buildings in question. Blame was immediately fixed on the Chechen rebels, and the Russian populace, unaccustomed to random violence and long used to random searches and strict police supervision of their lives, cried out for more controls. Talk of suspending the Constitution wafted through the government, and any dark-haired person with a North Caucasian nationality in their passport was, despite supposed equal citizenship rights, as suspect in Moscow as Japanese-Americans had been in coastal California in 1942.

Prime Minister Putin flew to the field headquarters of the Chechen conflict to rally the troops. Television cameras followed as drinks were passed for the obligatory round of toasting. But before glasses were raised to lips, in a dramatic bout of eloquence that riveted public opinion in his favor, the new leader slammed his glass on the table and announced that they would all drink – that was a certainty – but only later, after the work was done. The image of strength, resolve and articulate direction in this well-timed gesture seemed to seal his public mandate — provided he could deliver safety and security to the Russian people in short order.

CHAPTER 2

TRAVELLING THIRD CLASS

Yekaterinburg, Russia, September 4.

At 5:30 a.m. local time,[82] I stood on the platform in front of Car Number 5, clutching my 170-rouble *Platzkarta* ticket as the arriving passengers de-trained. Seven dollars to travel more than 1500 kilometers. Like a scene out of *Doctor Zhivago*, people were elbowing to be the first into the car, to call dibs on the few lower bunks left. Those poor souls stuck with an upper bunk would have to sit like hunchbacks during the day unless invited down by their lower-level car-mates.

Inside, the car was arranged in nine open cubicles of 6 bunks each, stacked two high. A third level, above, served as a luggage shelf. The *provodnitsa* came through collecting tickets, noting who would be sleeping in which space, and distributing packets of clean sheets and a towel in exchange for 11 roubles. There was a flurry of bed-making, then all was quiet save the clicking and jostling of the rails, the deep breathing and snoring of 54 passengers, and the odd baby crying.

An hour outside of Tyumen, another flurry of activity began, as disembarking passengers rolled up their bedding, shed their nylon track suits and slippers and donned chic meet-me-on-the-platform outfits. The train stopped; the passengers drained out; a new group flooded in, and the same transition happened in reverse. During the

---

82. Trains on the Trans-Siberian Railway, which pass through 8 time zones, are designated on the schedules and tickets in Moscow time. Yekaterinburg is two hours ahead of Moscow time. Due to the far northern latitude of the railway and the curvature of the earth, the time zones are not as broad as those in the United States.

momentary lull I snagged a lower bunk and happily straightened out my creaking neck.

A mustachioed man acquired the spot above me.

"Excuse me, do you suppose you could find a sheet of paper that I could wrap this in?" My new bunk-mate held out a greasy home-made *pirog* purchased on the platform.

I tore a page from my newspaper and handed it up.

"Thanks. I hope you already read that page. Here – you can read my book if you want." An arm reached down and he dropped a trashy paperback, also purchased on the platform, on the small table between the bunks.

The daytime travelling rhythm settled in. Toddlers wandered the corridor, picking up the slippers of sleeping passengers and dropping them randomly elsewhere. A woman stood in the corridor holding a large carrot and a kitchen grater, making carrot salad for breakfast. Families ate dark bread, sausage and tomatoes for breakfast, finishing the meal with tea drunk from canning jars filled at the coal-fired *samovar* at the end of the car. The *provodnitsa* came through and rousted a young man napping without rented sheets. "Roll up that mattress!"

The train rolled through flat swamplands, where tall grasses were interspersed by small birch trees and other hardwoods. Golden fall leaves were appearing. At Mangut, a tiny settlement west of Omsk, huge stacks of hay were stockpiled next to the railway line.

The train halted momentarily at small stations. A slow-moving freight train passed, heading eastward, its flat cars loaded with fully-built aluminum electrical sub-stations, living shacks and ancient cat-tracked army tanks, no doubt destined for a new retirement life as all-terrain vehicles somewhere in the swamps of Siberia.

At noon the mustachioed man above me awoke. Hungry in spite of the breakfast *pirog*, he tucked a bottle of vodka in his belt and went off to find the dining car. An hour later he returned with the bottle ⅔ empty.

"Man, was that expensive! I just spent 115 roubles for lunch, and I brought my own drinks. I was the only one in the dining car. The cook told me he buys potatoes here at 15 roubles for two buckets.[83] At that price, you would think he could charge a little less for a meal."

Victoria Ivanovna, on the opposite bunk, was a retired nurse from Tatarstan. She plied me with homegrown apples and tea.

"I don't have any sugar. Here, put some spoonfuls of homemade strawberry jam in the tea." She pulled out a canning jar and unscrewed the lid.

"I'm going to Sakhalin,[84] to where my parents used to live. It will take ten days to get there. Goodness, that's a long time to travel. In the old days, I could afford to fly and could get there in one day. Things were much better then. Now there has been such inflation that my pension is too small."

An ethnic Russian, Victoria Ivanovna spoke warmly of the Tatars, among whom she had lived for 30 years. "No, there are no ethnic tensions. The Russian children learn Tatar at school as well; it's we old folks who can't seem to get the language into our heads."

What did she think of the situation in Chechnya?

Of course she understood their desire for independence. She sat silently and looked out the window. A nurse sees the ugly side of war. Tears welled in her eyes and spilled down her cheeks. It was the end of the conversation.

---

83. Buckets, canning jars and glass tumblers are common units of measure used by peasants selling produce at the roadside, in train stations and in bazaars. The jars and tumblers are used for smaller edibles such as berries, sunflower seeds and pine nuts. Peasants who engage in trade more regularly often have a hand scale the size of an alarm clock to which they can hook the handles of a string bag to weigh items, but reading such a scale is a problem for peasants with poor eyesight, as most cannot afford glasses. Small merchants with regular vegetable stands use a two-sided scale with a series of hand weights.

84. Sakhalin is a large island on the Pacific coast just north of Japan. It was the site of the shooting down of Korean Air Lines Flight 007 by the Soviet air force on September 1, 1983.

CHAPTER 3

THE HEART OF
FLY-OVER COUNTRY

Novosibirsk, Russia, September 6.

A chill wind blew under gray skies. Open-air grocery kiosks were stacked high with plastic sacks of macaroni, and cafés offered *pelmeni* as their staple dish.

We seemed to be on a continental divide of sorts; a watershed between Europe and Asia, a borderline between burgers and *pen-se*. Toyotas from Japan, with steering wheels on the right, plied the streets, edging out Volkswagens as the used import car of choice. ("They're cheaper than the German cars," explained a taxi driver. "And as for the steering wheel? Pff! They drive the same.") The single television channel in Novosibirsk was running instant noodle ads, while German yogurt still held its place on store shelves. In the unthinkable vacuum of a flatlands city devoid of MacDonald's, Pizza Hut and nearly everything else Western, Russian fast food chains Grill-Master and Patio Pizza had taken up the flagship locations.

The metro stations of Novosibirsk were lined in a grand opulence of dark marble and granite. The main train station, grander still, was reminiscent of an international air terminal – clean, modern and well organized, with the sort of insulated corridors that bespeak a very harsh winter. The architecture of the central department store, however, was stuck somewhere between the '60s and the '70s.

Irkutsk, Russia, September 8.

Two nights and a day on the train from Novosibirsk brought me to Irkutsk. Inside half an hour, a bright sunny day became a dust storm swirling with fall leaves, followed closely by hail, then drenching rain while the sun still shone. Very strange. A weather pattern as complex and intricate as post-Communist Russian life itself.

Far from the devastation of World War II, the classical buildings of Irkutsk sat among Nineteenth Century wooden houses, ravaged only by the elements and by the indignities of encroaching Soviet architecture.

CHAPTER 4

SELF-RELIANT FAMILY AND NEIGHBORS

Listvyanka, Russia, September 10.

The bus driver dropped me off on the highway at the edge of Lake Baikal. [85] I hiked up the high hill behind the Limnological Museum to the Hotel *Baikal* and approached the front desk.

"Unfortunately we have no little rooms[86] available," the clerk told me sweetly. It was the only hotel in town.

"Do you know any other place in town to spend the night?"

"Just a moment." She picked up the telephone and gave the rotary dial a few spins.

"Nina Ivanovna, can you meet someone at the top of the stairs? Please decide for yourself, of course, whether you want to keep her or not."

She gave me directions back down the hill.

Half way down the hill, a plump sixty-something woman in trousers intercepted me and led the way down a set of sagging wooden steps and across a rotting plank walkway.

---

85. See sidebar *Lake Baikal*, page 169.

86. Diminutive forms of words are often used to convey warmth and informality.

Lake Baikal

The largest fresh-water lake in the world, formed 25 million years ago by the clashing of two tectonic plates, Lake Baikal is rimmed with snow-covered mountains even in early September. Despite the immense volume of water it contains (nearly twenty percent of the world's fresh water), because the lake is long, very deep and relatively narrow, it looks similar to Lake Tahoe on the California-Nevada border.

"Be careful – don't put your foot on that spot. The Institute used to take care of these steps, but now – watch out again – the Institute has moved to Irkutsk and these steps are in no man's land between the museum and the hotel. No one is responsible for taking care of them."

Before retiring, Nina Ivanovna had been a bookkeeper for the local government, in charge of school and public works finances. Her late husband had been a ship captain on Lake Baikal, hauling passengers and supplies, including the materials to build a new railway line through the Taiga at the north end of the lake. Now retired and recently widowed, Nina Ivanovna had turned over their small wooden house and garden to her son's family. Her son, through savings from a stint as a sailor, had bought a two-room apartment for her on the hill behind the Limnological Museum.

"This is a much better place for a pensioner. The house was a lot of work. We always had to haul wood and coal. Here I have steam heat."

I took my shoes off at the door as usual.

"Sorry, the light in the water closet [87] doesn't work. There's something wrong with the wiring, but my son can't fix it right now because he broke his leg. I called the fix-it man from the museum but he

---

87. In Soviet-built apartments, the toilet is often in a tiny room by itself, while the tub and sink are in a separate room next to it. An invention found in many apartment and hotel bathrooms is a faucet with a long spout that can be swung back and forth between the sink and the tub. While perhaps slightly more inconvenient than having separate faucets for each fixture, the device allowed the Soviet-era plumbing factories to turn out enough faucets to outfit twice the number of apartments.

wasn't at work today." [88]

"How did your son break his leg?"

"Falling out of a pine tree. He was gathering cones. [89] They had to operate and put a pin in his leg. He spent two months in the hospital and finally came home today. Now he will spend another month in a cast and be off work for another three months after that — half a year altogether."

She sliced a tomato and a cucumber, salted them heavily and put them on a small plate on the table.

"We were lucky. It could have been much worse. He is *alive*. He will recover. We pensioners need our children in order to survive; they are our hope. I, too, was in the hospital recently. My son helped me a lot. He bought me medicine; it's very expensive now. The woman next to me did not have any relatives to buy her medicine. She simply died."

Nina Ivanovna filled the electric *samovar* with water, plugged it in, spooned loose tea leaves into a small metal teapot, filled the pot with boiling water and balanced it in the small hollow on top of the *samovar*.[90]

"Still, it's not easy with my son laid up," she continued. "In addition to his job, he has a small tractor and earns extra money harvesting potatoes from other people's garden plots."

"Oh, he has a small *biznes*," I commended.

"No, no!" She reproached me sternly, sitting up straighter and

---

88. Use of the company fix-it man to fix a problem in an individual's apartment in the community falls in a large gray area somewhere between a personal favor and a fringe benefit to a company employee or pensioner. Company spare parts will be used, to the extent accessible. No money will change hands and there may be no direct *quid pro quo* at the time. However, a favor will generally be exchanged at some point in a good neighborly fashion.

89. Pine nuts are a Siberian delicacy.

90. This is the traditional way Russians make tea. After the leaves in the small teapot steep, the thick brew is poured into the teacup according to taste, then boiling water is added to fill the cup. Most Russians like several heaping spoonfuls of sugar in a cup of tea. Tea is not served until the end of the meal.

shaking her finger. "That's not *biznes*; that's work." [91]

"What's the difference?"

"*Biznes* is exploitation; it's not honorable."

"Always?"

"Always. If all you do is go to Moscow to buy goods for a low price and sell them here for a high price, that's not work – it's speculation."

"But there is work involved. The trader has to spend money for gas, train tickets and so forth to get the goods here."

"I don't object to that."

"And there is risk involved. If the trader brings melons from Astrakhan, they may spoil before they get here."

"That's OK too. He should earn something for that. But to earn *ten times* more? That's exploitation. I can't afford to buy his melons with my pension."

"We don't have many people in the United States making tenfold profit by trading. As soon as a retailer did that, someone else would come along and sell the same goods for nine times more, then yet another for eight, until pretty soon there would be little profit left." I wasn't going to bring Microsoft into the discussion.

"It doesn't happen that way here. There are barriers keeping other people out of the market. Before, we all lived at the same economic level. Now, twenty per cent of the population is living very well. The rest of us are just scraping by. Look at this table. Everything on it except the bread and the sugar came from our garden, and if I need to I can make my own bread, too. People survive here on what they grow in their garden plots; on hunting and fishing, or smoking fish and selling it at the roadside."

She retrieved three kinds of Siberian berries from the giant deep freezer in her hallway and put them in a cut glass dish for me to sample.

"But we are lucky. City people who are out of work have it much worse. And there are problems in the making which are only going to manifest themselves much later. Many children are not going to school. Our buildings are getting older and older."

---

91. She used the word *trud*, literally 'work' or 'labor.' During Soviet times, *trud* was a word that featured heavily in large billboards praising the socialist revolution.

She spoke warmly and enthusiastically of the Stalin years. "*Oh, we were strong then!* Things kept getting better and better all the time. We built factories, airplanes. We were a world power. We had our fill of bread, of vegetables. Stalin honored the *Stakhanovtsi.*" Her entire posture had changed. She sat up straight as she spoke, clenching her fist.

"Of course, there were many things he did that were improper. He had his dalliances, and it wasn't right sending people off to the *GULAG* without a trial. But he ruled with an iron hand, and as a result *we were great*. The country has been going downhill ever since he died. Khrushchev, Brezhnev – they were weak. The only strong leader we've had since Stalin was Yuri Andropov. He did not put up with any foolishness. People were not running around shopping during work hours any more. They were sitting at their desks working! If he hadn't been killed so soon, things might have gotten better."

"Killed?"

"Yes, it was a contract assassination."

"It wasn't reported that way in the West."

"Every Russian knows that's what happened.[92] They got away with it because he was an old man. Khrushchev and Brezhnev were allowed to live to a natural death – they were malleable enough that the powers-that-be simply used them to do what they wanted, just as Boris Nikolaevich [93] is a puppet."

"Would you agree to live under Stalinism again?"

"*In an instant.*"

---

92. I have found no Western source to corroborate this assertion and render no opinion as to whether it is true or false. It may be the product of an active rumor mill which developed over the years in the absence of a free press, and through which things came to be considered true simply by being widely disseminated through unofficial channels. Andropov was in poor health long before his death and could easily have died of natural causes. But it is also a fact that Andropov was replaced with the equally ailing, but less reform-minded, Konstantin Chernenko. Andropov protégé Mikhail Gorbachev was not allowed to ascend to the highest office at that point. Thus, the rumor is supported at least by a corroborating motive.

93. Boris Yeltsin. Nikolaevich is his patronymic.

CHAPTER 5

SCHOOLTEACHERS TURNED FISH-MONGERS

Listvyanka, Russia, September 12.

I planned a day trip to the near-ghost village of Port Baikal, a short ferry ride along Lake Baikal from Listvyanka. Port Baikal was formerly a center of activity, barging train cars across the lake. Later, it was a stop on the beautiful section of the Trans-Siberian Railway traversing the shoreline of Lake Baikal. In 1956 it was virtually cut off from the rest of the world by the building of a reservoir on the Angara River, which flooded the tracks between Irkutsk and Port Baikal.

I lingered over breakfast in Nina Ivanovna's kitchen. One by one, she cheerfully tossed nearly a dozen delicious crepe-thin *blinchiki* hot out of the pan and onto my plate, where I topped each one with homemade raspberry preserves.[94]

I had decided to flag down a car for an informal taxi ride instead of catching the bus down to the ferry, four kilometers away in the village. It turned out to be a near-mistake – it was Sunday morning and there was virtually no traffic. When I reached the main road at the bottom of the hill, I made another tactical mistake: picking and choosing the cars to flag down.

The first vehicle that happened by was a tank truck; the second was an ambulance. I let them both pass; it seemed inappropriate to divert them from their official duties. A 15-minute break followed with no traffic at all in the direction of the village. Meanwhile, the ambulance came back in the other direction, dropping three girls off

---

94. Maple syrup is unknown in Russia. Local residents tap birch trees for sap, but the liquid is generally consumed as juice rather than being boiled down into syrup.

across the street, and the tank truck whizzed by behind it, also carrying a passenger. Time to start walking. Half way to the village, I finally caught a ride from the next car to pass, a Toyota with a steering wheel on the right-hand side.

By the time the ferry docked in Listvyanka on the return trip from Port Baikal, a storm had whipped up and a cold wind was blowing. A dozen portable iron stoves were smoking away in the parking lot. Stacks of kindling were piled nearby. Villagers bundled in many layers of clothing were baking *omul*, a trout-like fish from the lake. A woman in a wool cap pulled one off the grill and plopped it into a plastic bag for me, where it warmed my freezing hands. I quickly consumed it.

Nina Ivanovna returned home that evening with a bouquet of orange tiger lilies, yellow carnations and magenta cosmos from her garden patch. The last for the year, she thought; frost was forecast for Irkutsk that night.

"Let me bake an *omul* for you for dinner, please."

"Sure!"

"Did you catch a ride all right this morning?"

I explained the minor difficulties. "What is that truck with a tank on the back? I must have seen it a dozen times today."

"Oh, that's the sewer truck. You should have stopped him; he's our alternate bus service. Whenever we've missed the bus, he stops for us. I used to be able to hop up into his cab so easily. Now I'm getting old."

The baked *omul* appeared on the table, filleted, sprinkled with shredded carrots and strips of onion, and accompanied by slices of fried potatoes and a salad made from shredded cabbage, chunks of tomato and cucumber, sliced green onion and dill.

"Tasty."

"It would be even tastier if you had let me spread mayonnaise on it," she chided me.[95]

---

95. Both Russians and Ukrainians are fond of large quantities of mayonnaise, which is frequently used as a salad dressing over shredded cabbage, shredded carrots, shredded cooked beets or other vegetables.

Nina Ivanovna told me that all the doctors and all the teachers in the community were now small-time fish merchants; it was the only way they could feed their families, due to the long delays in receiving their meager official salaries, which had not kept up with inflation. She also talked about the environment around the lake, and the pulp mill dumping chemicals across the lake.

"Lot's of people in Listvyanka die of cancer. That's what took my husband, too. He was only 60. They say it's in the rocks around here. The fish and seal populations have gone way down. Berries and mushrooms used to be much more plentiful, too. People are yanking the mushrooms out by the roots instead of slicing them off. That way they don't grow back."

Nina Ivanovna's son had been taken back to the hospital earlier in the day. He had fallen down the porch steps at home and re-injured his leg.

CHAPTER 6

THE UNCULTURED PEASANT

Listvyanka, Russia, September 13.

Being an avid swimmer, there was one piece of unfinished business to take care of before I left Lake Baikal: a dip in the lake. With a chilly wind and leaden skies, I would need a place to warm up within spitting distance of the frigid water. The answer was the *banya* next to the meteorological station at the mouth of the Angara River.

Nina Ivanovna and I tried the owners' 3-digit telephone number again and again, but there was no answer, so I walked over to see what could be arranged. Port Baikal was a stone's throw away across the mouth of the Angara River, the only outlet for the water from this giant lake. The surface of the river mouth was riffled in mid-stream, where the momentum picked up and the water began its descent toward Irkutsk. Nina Ivanovna had warned me about the strong current, which had recently taken the life of a young man.

In the workshop of the house next door to the meteorological station I found a slight, weatherbeaten old man wearing knee-high rubber boots and a sheepskin-lined vest. He seemed pleased to have a female cross his field of vision, and immediately set about being helpful. First, he grasped a large butcher knife from his workbench, cut a thick slice of bread off a new loaf and, pressing it into my hands, indicated that I was to feed it to his largest dog as a peace offering.

"The owner of the *banya* is gone until tomorrow. But I have the key. Come, I'll show you."

He led the way down a long steep flight of wooden steps to the beach.

"Is that sidecar motorcycle yours?"

"Naw. I just live here quietly now. I don't need to go anywhere. I have my work; everything I need. My family left me long ago." He was 56 years old, but looked a full generation older. Strings of obscenities cheerfully emanated from his mouth.

We reached the *banya*, a tiny green and white wooden cottage on the beach. We climbed the porch steps.

"I hope the dog isn't inside," he said, struggling with the lock. "I'm afraid of it."

"Here, let me help you." I turned the key right side up, reinserted it in the lock and began to wiggle it around. My host took advantage of the break to clear his throat loudly and spit a generous wad over the railing.

The lock turned and I opened the door a crack. Two large eyes met mine.

"The dog's there!" I slammed the door, re-locked it and thanked him. We went back up the hill.

A well-fed, double-chinned neighbor had happened by and was looking down on us from the top of the steps, hands shoved in the pockets of a handsome leather coat. When he heard why we had locked the door again, he wouldn't hear of letting the little old man be such a coward.

"That dog's not so bad," he jeered. "Go back down; call the dog to you. Everything will be all right."

We went back down the stairs and undid the lock again. The weathered old man started calling in a low soothing voice. I carefully opened the door. An enormous German Shepherd sprang out and, without a sound, trotted down the beach.

"It's enough to make you wet your pants, isn't it?" my host commented.

Inside, there was a wood-fired sauna, a small sleeping area, a table filled with teacups, a window with an icon over it, a stuffed elk head, a silent cuckoo clock, and a sink basin which functioned only with the aid of a pair of buckets (one above and one below.) The little man built a fire in the stove of the sauna, fetched a bucket of cold water from the lake to make steam, showed me how to open the iron stove door with a canvas mitt to add wood, and cut me a fresh bunch of birch leaves.[96] The dog returned quietly and lay down on the bed.

"There, now, if you have everything you need, I'll leave now. Enjoy yourself, only no lying with the dog!"

---

96. Young birch branches with fresh green leaves are used to flail oneself and one's neighbor while sweating in the sauna.

CHAPTER 7

HITCHHIKING TO IRKUTSK

After three wonderful days, it was time to say goodbye to Nina Ivanovna and return to Irkutsk to catch the train eastward.

Mid-way between Listvyanka and Irkutsk was an Architectural Museum of traditional houses.

"Flag down any car," Nina Ivanovna advised. "Have them drop you at the museum, then catch the evening bus to Irkutsk when it passes through."

Nina Ivanovna nearly collapsed in gratitude when she counted the green American banknotes I gave her for the lodging. "Now I can buy medicine for my son!"

I picked up my pack, walked down the hill to the main road, and stuck my hand out. The first car pulled over. I squeezed into the back seat and we breezed through gently rolling hills, looking for the museum turnoff in the woods.

"Stop! We just passed it," called the other passenger, pointing to a sign 200 yards back. I jumped out and thanked them.

As the car swished away over the next hill, I was left in utter silence on the desolate road. I shouldered the pack and strolled back to read the sign.

'Welcome to the National Park,' it read. No museum here.

I spied another sign, half a mile further, and started hiking.

'Tour Base – Closed.'[97] Still no museum. I'd better flag down another car.

The tires of a four-seater covered Army jeep hummed over the quiet roadway, growing louder. I stuck my hand out and the jeep swerved over. I jumped into the front seat and exchanged friendly greetings with three handsome young men inside.

---

97. Tour buses, or *turbazi*, are very primitive accommodations in which Russians stay to enjoy a vacation in the great outdoors.

"Where are you from?"

"America."

The driver practically slammed on the brakes in astonishment.

"*How* on earth did you get *here*?"

They speculated that I must have fallen out of the sky, and that my backpack was really a parachute.

"*I'd* be *afraid* to travel alone in *America*," continued the driver.

"With good reason. America's a scary place."

I certainly wouldn't be hitchhiking like this at home, but this was still a semi-closed society and I was on a dead-end road from a small town where the townspeople all knew their neighbors.

Two kilometers further down the road we found the real museum, and I disappeared out of their lives as quickly as I had fallen in.

PART VII

TRANS-SIBERIAN RAILROAD - EAST

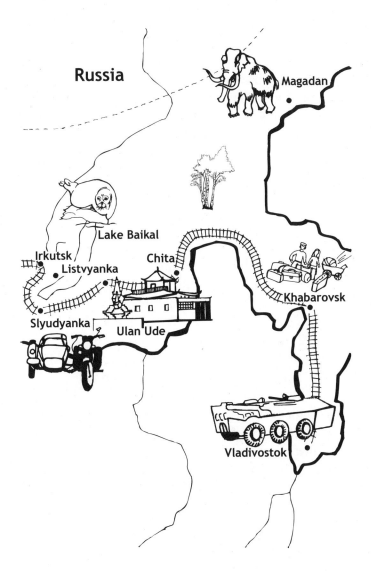

Russia

Magadan

Lake Baikal

Irkutsk   Chita
Listvyanka

Slyudyanka   Ulan Ude

Khabarovsk

Vladivostok

CHAPTER 1

SCIENTISTS
RIDING THE RAILS

Irkutsk, Russia, September 14.

I boarded the train for Ulan Ude. Though it would be a day trip for me, the long-distance train pulled only sleeping cars. I was assigned to a compartment in which two men were just waking up. I stowed my pack in the compartment, then waited in the corridor while they pulled the sheets off their bunks, rolled up their mattresses and changed out of their nylon track suits.

"We're scientists from Novosibirsk," they said. "We've come to study the water quality in Lake Baikal."

Packed in their gym bags along with the usual assortment of tomatoes, sausages and hard-boiled eggs were bottles of water-testing chemicals.

"Flying is expensive, but I think this is the last time we will ride 33 hours on the train [each way] for a business trip."

The train pulled into Slyudyanka, an industrial town on the southern shore of the lake. A large scar gashed the mountainside above, bleeding mounds of whitish dirt.

"That's where they mine *slyuda*," said Oleg, the younger of the two scientists. "It's an excellent insulator against high voltage electricity, but it's nearly as carcinogenic as asbestos."

The two scientists got off in the town of Baikalsk, and the train left the lake shore to travel eastward. Snow-covered mountains appeared in the distance, behind golden birch trees and patches of green grass. It seemed that Shangri La would be around the corner any minute now.

CHAPTER 2

BURYAT SENIOR CITIZENS

Ulan Ude, Republic of Buryatia, Russia, September 15.

I decided to ride the twelve o'clock #104 bus out to Ivolginsk to see the Buddhist *datsan* (temple). But when I arrived at the bus station parking lot, the Buryat version of a Volkswagen-stuffing contest was under way on the bus in question. Two elderly women armed with groceries were energetically shoving with their backs into the bottlenecked entryway, carrying on loud, cheerful bantering monologues.

"Come on, there *must* be a little more room in the center aisle. Granny can't go without her cart!" The two-wheel grocery carrier was still hanging from her hands, in thin air below the bus step.

Finally the bus driver came around and took the cart to put in the driver's cab. He gave the human cargo half a dozen extra shoves, and with great effort, by hand, closed the crooked folding doors around them.

Another five Buryat senior citizens were standing more sedately on the tarmac, either having decided that the sardine-pack was not for them, or recognizing the physical impossibility of squeezing in even one more human being. The next #104 bus was due in four hours, but the locals knew about a *marshrutnoye* leaving from the other bus station, a kilometer away, so we all paraded over there. *Baba* Zhenia, an elderly Buryat woman already bundled in a scarf and boots against the frosty mid-September cold, was going to the *datsan* too, to consult an astrologer there, and took me under her wing to make sure I found my way.

Buryatia

The Buryats have carved a semi-autonomous republic out of the wind-swept prairies east of Lake Baikal. In the capital, Ulan Ude, Mongolian features predominate on the streets and in the shops. (Buryats are related to Mongolians.) East of the city are pine groves. To the west, the wilderness feels like somewhere near Cheyenne, Wyoming, with rolling steppe and distant hills.

The ancient dark wooden houses on the old streets of Ulan Ude have fancy carved wooden shutters and window frames like those in western Russia, but with strongly Buddhist curves.

Chapter 3

The Frisky Nurse

Ulan Ude, Republic of Buryatia, Russia, September 15.

Rosa, a 25-year-old Tatar nurse from Irkutsk, was vacationing in Ulan Ude, staying with relatives in town.

"In the mornings, I go to the hospital and work. No, they don't pay me. I just like to help out with the operations. You should *see* the operating rooms: they have all the equipment and supplies they need — just like on the American television shows! And they have sinks where the water turns on just by putting your hand under the faucet."

Rosa, who had until recently enjoyed an intimate relationship with a married doctor in Irkutsk, couldn't understand why President Clinton had had to talk about his sex life in public. "It seems to me that it's a private matter between him and Monica."

I explained how the President's sex life had become an issue through the Paula Jones suit, and why we had sexual harassment laws in America.

Rosa shook her head in puzzlement. "How can you have laws against that? It's impossible — it's human nature for men to behave like that. Besides, I can't imagine any woman *not* wanting that kind of attention."

I explained the obstruction of justice issues surrounding the Clinton case. This was still more incomprehensible to Rosa.

"But laws are *meant* to be avoided," she protested.

CHAPTER 4

THE LONGEST LEG
OF THE JOURNEY

Ulan Ude, Republic of Buryatia, Russia, September 16.

In every marathon, there comes a point when one "hits the wall." Perhaps that is too strong an expression for the 52-hour passage between Ulan Ude and Khabarovsk. But every once in a while, I got the sense that the Russian National Railroad had sent a *provodnitsa* to test my patience.

Boarding in Ulan Ude, I found myself in a compartment with two nice Russian women and an old Portuguese man who spoke little English. I had drawn a top bunk when I purchased my ticket, considered less desirable than a lower bunk even in a *kupé*, where it was possible to sit upright during the day on any bunk. But no matter — I was an expert by now at squeezing my pack into the luggage space above the doorway and arranging water, food and toiletries on the small shelf above the bunk. I had everything in order by the time the *provodnitsa* came around to check tickets.

"Come with me," she ordered.

I dropped down off the top bunk, slipped on my shoes and followed her to the compartment next door, which was completely empty.

"Choose any bunk you like here."

186

Boy, was it my lucky day. I chose the lower one facing forward, and she tucked my ticket into the corresponding pocket of her organizer.

"Now," she continued, "can you explain to the other American in your compartment that he can move in here as well? That way, you can keep him company."

"He's not American – he's Portuguese. Besides, I came here to meet *Russians*." I was getting the feeling that the foreigners were being isolated and ghetto-ized.

"But he doesn't speak Russian, and he won't have anyone to visit with if he stays in there."

"Oh, all right." He was only riding to Chita, nine hours away. *Provodnitsas* could make your life pleasant or unpleasant, and it wouldn't hurt to be on her good side. Had I any idea what was to follow, I would not have been such a good sport.

After nine hours of halting English the Portuguese man took his leave at Chita. I gratefully made my bed on one of the lower bunks, crawled under the clean sheets and rough wool blanket, and went to sleep. The respite was brief.

At a small village on the outskirts of Chita the train shuddered to a stop. In the darkness, heavy footsteps came down the corridor and the door to my compartment slid open. A lanky, chiseled frame in dark clothing, work boots and an orange vest was outlined in the dim corridor light. Behind him I heard scuffling and hushed staccato voices. Heavy suitcases were brought in, then more. And more. The beam of the railwayman's powerful flashlight swung round the tiny compartment as wiry arms hoisted the heavy bags into the luggage space above the door and crammed them under the lower bunks. Then came a baby carriage, and finally a young couple with a one-year-old toddler in tow. For the next 36 hours, the toddler loudly an incessantly expressed his disappointment with the travelling conditions.

The toddler was travelling with his mother and his young uncle, Dima. Dima worked for the railroad, so he could make the 72-hour round trip journey for free to pick up his sister and nephew and bring them back to live with him in a village in the middle of Siberia.

"I love winter when it's nice and cold," he gushed, reminiscing about hunting trips and long winter nights in the *banya* with friends. "Life is good in our small town."

The train made a provision stop in another town where life was not so good. While train personnel clamped large hoses to hydrants beside the tracks to refill the train's WC tanks and the baggage car workers unloaded cases of pink and green soda pop in plastic bottles for the village store, dirty-faced children came in droves to beg for bread. A few of the village adults walked the length of the train trying to sell pine cones and buckets of tiny berries.

"There are a lot of ex-prisoners living in exile out here," said Dima, "Many of the parents are alcoholics. They have nothing — no jobs, no education, no hope."

After a few more hours of wailing and whining, the toddler, his family and baggage were left standing by the train tracks near their village, and I was blissfully alone in the four-bed compartment.

Twenty minutes later, at the next town, the *provodnitsa* assigned me two new fellow travelers – a nerd and a bum. The former settled quietly in to a pile of magazines. The latter immediately fell asleep on the upper bunk, reeking of alcohol and unwashed human being, his grubby bare toes dangling over the edge of the bed. Even with the door open, the third passenger to be assigned to the compartment quickly backed out. A moment later the *provodnitsa* appeared.

"I thought there was a free bunk in here," she said accusingly, looking crossly at us.

An hour before arrival time my upstairs neighbor roused himself and wandered off somewhere. The *provodnitsa* brought my cancelled ticket back[98] and collected my sheets and towel.

"Well, I trust you had a pleasant trip."

I said nothing at all.

---

98. See sidebar *Dead Souls*, page 189.

Dead Souls

Every provodnitsa keeps the passengers' torn ticket stubs during the journey and comes around offering to return them at the end. Once, when I motioned to the provodnitsa that I didn't need the stub back, one of my compartment mates chastised me: "Why did you turn it down? You could have sold it." It turned out that there was a market for used ticket stubs. Those who wished to take a day off work and claim they had gone on a business trip could simply go to the train station, meet the train returning from their purported destination, purchase a torn stub from a disembarking passenger, and turn it in at their place of work for expense reimbursement. In Odessa, Ukraine, tram conductors sell tickets to passengers with only a slight cancellation tear. It is considered a gesture of kindness for the passenger to return the ticket to the conductor at the end of the trip, so that the same ticket can be sold to another passenger. This enables the conductor to supplement her meager salary.

Chapter 5

The Russian Far East

Khabarovsk, Russia, September 19.

It felt good to sleep in a bed that wasn't moving, to walk the streets in the fresh air and to have a shower. The latter was bracing — no hot water in this town, either, though the light in the bathroom worked this time. Light bulbs seemed to be in short supply all along the Trans-Siberian route.

Breakfast was loaded into the room price again, so I went down to see what it was. *Kashmar* – a disaster – would be the best way to describe it. Lascivious heavy metal lyrics were echoing through the nearly-empty dining room. It was hard to tell whether the young waitress was oblivious to the meaning of the English obscenities in the music or clueless as to normal standards of good taste.

As the graphic chorus of the song reverberated through the room a second time, the waitress returned and dumped a plate in front of me piled with stinking, steaming cabbage, a boiled wiener squirted with thin ketchup, rice and a roll with a slab of butter. I informed her that the music selection was not appropriate for breakfast. She looked puzzled, but found another tape. My appetite did not return, but the rice was edible and the tea drinkable.

Khabarovsk was a 'big city,' with a well-populated main street and lots of cafés. I bought a copy of *Dengi* ("Money"), a weekly magazine. The cover was torn. I handed the kiosk attendant a torn ten-rouble note. It seemed a fair exchange to me, but she didn't think so.

"Hey, give me different *dengi*," she barked.

I finally unloaded the torn note on the hotel desk clerk, who checked with her colleague before accepting it.[99]

My project for the day was to buy a plane ticket home. There were lots of airline ticket offices, and they all seemed to be open, even on Sunday. But it took a few visits to find one that sold international tickets.

There seemed to be only two possibilities to the United States out of Vladivostok: Korean Airlines and Aeroflot. Alaska Airlines, I was told, had closed up shop a year earlier. And it was impossible to buy a ticket on Korean Airlines, or even obtain any information about its schedule, in Khabarovsk. So I bought a ticket on Aeroflot.

The really good news was that the ticket agent accepted credit cards. The bad news was that the cashier was at lunch. When she finally returned, it took another 45 minutes to assemble the necessary paperwork. I was their first MasterCard customer ever, it turned out, and each step in the instruction manual had to be confirmed by telephone with the head of the office, at home on a Sunday. The ticket tax had to be paid separately in cash.

---

99. In Russia, tearing is the main means of canceling tickets, etc. People are particularly meticulous about the quality of money, and suspicious of counterfeiting. Money that has accidentally made a trip through the washing machine might as well be thrown away.

CHAPTER 6

ALL FOREIGNERS ARE ALIKE

Khabarovsk, Russia, September 20.

The trip from Khabarovsk to Vladivostok would be my nineteenth and last night on the train. I had to buy a "foreigner's" ticket, which was identical to an ordinary Russian ticket but with a paper cover stapled over it. The *provodnitsa* found me a lower bunk with quite ordinary Russian citizens. We had hot tea and settled in for a quiet night — save one small interruption. As I was drifting off to sleep with the rhythmic jouncing of the car against the rails, the *provodnitsa* barged in with an urgent question.

"Say, you're a foreigner. Can you tell me what this is for?" She bent down near my bunk, holding out a tiny box. I roused myself and snapped on the reading light above my pillow. The box was labeled in French. Inside was a screw-topped vial with perfumed talc. I explained what it was for and how to wear it.

"You mean all it does is smell good?"

"Yes."

She went merrily back to her *provodnitsa* compartment and I went back to sleep. 'Foreigners,' whether Portuguese, French or American, seemed to be interchangeable in the eyes of the *provodnitsi*.

Tea on the Train

Passengers in Platzkarte save money by bringing their own loose tea or tea bags and a mug with them on the train and filling up with hot water from the samovar. But the travelling middle and upper classes in kupé and lux like to have tea brought to them by the provodnitsa. For a pittance, hot tea is served elegantly in a tall glass in a fancy metal holder with a handle, accompanied by large packets of sugar.

192

Chapter 7

The End of the Line

Vladivostok, Russia, September 21.

I had reached the end of the line – the Pacific Ocean. No longer did the train station have two schedules posted: one east, one west. From here, all trains went west.

Amurski Bay would make any San Franciscan feel at home. The sun set over Marin County-like hills, complete with a small-scale Mount Tamalpais-shaped hump near the water. A stiff breeze blew through the coastal shrubbery, while windsurfers in wetsuits skipped along the shore. The heavy artillery of the Russian Pacific Fleet was moored around the point, in Golden Horn Bay.

Chapter 8

Souvenirs With a Hidden Price Tag

Vladivostok, Russia, September 23.

The gift shop at the Hotel *Vladivostok* was well stocked with souvenirs – amber necklaces, silk scarves, carvings from walrus and mammoth ivory, and brightly painted, lacquered nesting wooden *matryoshka* dolls.

"Where does the mammoth ivory come from?" I asked the clerk.

"From Magadan in the far North. There's a huge gold mine up there, and when the miners start digging, mammoths are sometimes found trapped in the ice."

"Can it be exported?"

"Yes, but you need a special export certificate." For about $10, such a certificate, an official instruction to the local customs agent to look the other way, could be in my hands in about 24 hours.

"And how about importing it into the United States?"

"Oh, that's not allowed. But don't worry: we have several customers who successfully take ivory to America regularly. Just don't declare it."

I thanked her and left without making a purchase, hoping the few other Americans who found their way to this land's end would also view the carving of paleontological history into tourist trinkets as too sacrilegious to support.[100]

---

100. The lacquered wooden *matryoshka* dolls probably came with their own silent baggage as well. A young businessman in Ukraine who was exporting lovely hand-painted eggs to the United States confided that he might not be able to keep up the highly profitable trade much longer. His artisans, it seemed, working for a pittance in a small studio, were catching on to the fact that the toxic fumes of the cheap oil-based paints were affecting their health.

Chapter 9

Coming Home

Vladivostok, Russia, September 24.

I took a suburban train to a whistle stop at the edge of Vladivostok, and tramped around the mud-puddles in the pocked pavement and up the embankment to the edge of the highway, where a local bus picked me up, along with the other passengers heading for the Vladivostok airport.

The international departure tax was collected in cash, and the young man who stamped my passport paid no attention whatsoever to the fact that my visa was unregistered or to the sizeable collection of hotel stamps – minus the *Astrakhanskaya* – I had so carefully collected in my visa.

After a short hop to pick up more passengers in Khabarovsk, the once-a-week Aeroflot flight winged its way eastward into the darkness toward Alaska, carrying a human cargo of roughneck oil and gas workers, American couples with Russian toddlers in tow, and a handful of missionaries and aid workers. There was no in-flight movie, but we were fed, and after a stop in Anchorage we were delivered safely to Seattle.

My burly Russian seat-mates headed for the docks to catch a fishing vessel. I wandered over to an airport espresso bar and gazed in wonder at the cascade of fresh-baked pastries under polished glass.

"Can I get you something?"

I sighed. "Still deciding."

It was going to take a while to come home.

About the Author

MOLLY J. BAIER is an attorney in San Francisco. She holds a degree in Russian Studies from Cornell College, and in Law from the University of California, Davis. Fluent in Russian and German, she lived in Kiev, Ukraine from 1997 to 1999, working for the American and British governments in aid of Ukraine's conversion from a communist to a capitalist system of laws. Ms. Baier is a member of the World Affairs Council of  Northern California, and of the International Diplomacy Council, for which she hosts USAID and State Department-sponsored visitors from Russia and other parts of the former Soviet Union.

About the Illustrator

LISA JACYSZYN is an artist of Ukrainian heritage.
A graduate of California College of Arts & Crafts, she lives and draws in Oakland, California.